MORE

Splendid Desserts

Recipes with No Sugar Added

Jennifer Eloff

Macmillan Canada

Toronto

Canadian Cataloguing in Publication Data

Eloff, Jennifer, 1957–

More splendid desserts : recipes with no sugar added

Includes index.
ISBN 0-7715-7428-2

1. Desserts.   2. Sugar-free diet – Recipes.
3. Low-calorie diet – Recipes.   I. Title.

TX773.E46 1997   641.8'6   C97–930322–2

Macmillan Canada wishes to thank the Canada Council, the Ontario Ministry of Culture and Communications and the Ontario Arts Council for supporting its publishing program.

This book is available at special discounts for bulk purchases by your group or organization for sales promotions, premiums, fundraising and seminars. For details, contact: Macmillan Canada, Special Sales Department, 29 Birch Avenue, Toronto, ON M4V 1E2. Tel: 416-963-8830

Cover and interior design: Gord Robertson
Cover and interior photos: Lothar Ulrich, Quebecor Studio
Food stylist: Rosemarie Superville
Pictured on cover: Peach Melba Chiffon Cake, page 28

Macmillan Canada
A Division of Canada Publishing Corporation
Toronto, Ontario, Canada

1 2 3 4 5 WC 01 00 99 98 97

Printed in Canada

Contents

ACKNOWLEDGMENTS

This book is dedicated with love and humble thankfulness to God, who was th source of my inspiration and whose guidance helped me fulfill a dream of bein able to help others.

My appreciation and thanks go to the many people involved in the support net work surrounding this book. I would like to thank:

Everyone at McNeil Consumer Products Company (a Johnson & Johnson company) in Canada for their enthusiasm, encouragement and support;

Everyone at McNeil Specialty Products Company (a Johnson & Johnson company) in the U.S.A. for their enthusiasm and encouragement;

Everyone at Macmillan for their kindness, professionalism and belief in this project, and especially my editor Nicole de Montbrun who worked very closely with me through the various stages;

Bev Renahan for the expert editing of my recipes;

Photographer Lothar Ulrich, Quebecor Studio and food stylist Rosemarie Superville for producing such beautiful photographs;

Sue Bailey (PHEc), Home Economics Consultant who tested several recipes and assisted with the editing of my manuscript;

Everyone at Info Access (1988) Inc. who prepared the expert nutrient analysis of the recipes;

Katherine Younker, PDt, CDE, Contract Dietitian for the Canadian Diabetes Association for the expert assignment of Food Choice Values and/or Symbols to recipes;

Those of my family and friends who contributed recipe ideas;

Lastly, but very importantly, many grateful, loving thanks to my family; my husband Ian and sons, Daniel and Jonathan, always the ever-willing tasters, for the blessing of their unselfish sacrifices, their patience, loving support and encouragement and for my husband's financial support.

* * *

I wish to thank and acknowledge LifeScan (a Johnson & Johnson company), "Canada's leader in blood glucose management for people with diabetes" as a corporate sponsor.

Introduction

My husband can't tolerate sugar!

This used to be a problem because if he couldn't eat desserts then I wouldn't bake them as often, so my entire family was deprived.

Seeking an alternative to baking with sugar, I researched many of the options on the low-calorie sweetener market—all were unsuitable for use in my baking, except SPLENDA® Granular.

SPLENDA® Low-Calorie Sweetener is a more natural sugar substitute because it is *created* from sugar. But, unlike sugar's 800 calories, it has a mere 100 calories per cup. A combination of sucralose and maltodextrin (a carbohydrate derived from corn, which provides the calories but which also allows it to measure like sugar), it is a chemically inert sugar substitute suitable for cooking and baking due to its incredible heat stability. Thanks to SPLENDA®, I am now able to make desserts without sugar added that closely resemble the real thing in taste, in texture and in appearance.

During the development of my two dessert books (*Splendid Desserts* and *More Splendid Desserts*), and over a four-year period, my family has consumed more than 5,000 cups of SPLENDA® without any ill effects. The results of more than 140 safety and environmental studies, over a period of 17 years, have shown that sucralose does not contribute to cardiovascular disease, cancer or genetic damage, and that it has no effect on the nervous system.

When I first started baking with SPLENDA® Granular, I quickly realized that to get the best results I had to do more than simply substitute SPLENDA® for sugar. SPLENDA® Granular has very little density (weighing ⅛ as much as sugar) and therefore imparts less structure and volume to baked items than sugar does. To duplicate the density and volume of sugar-rich desserts, I had to do some experimenting. I met with success and you'll find the delicious results in this cookbook.

Within *More Splendid Desserts* are recipes that all use SPLENDA® Low-Calorie Sweetener. I've also incorporated other low-calorie and low-fat ingredients. There is quite a range of desserts, from the really light and low-calorie through to the more luscious desserts that are heavier in calories and in fat. Overall, I took a moderate approach when cutting back on fat because a drastic reduction often produces an inferior result. Great taste was my first consideration and if that meant a few extra grams of fat per serving, I felt it was a worthy sacrifice.

Generally, however, my desserts are much lower in fat and calories than regular desserts (see comparison on page 54). Higher fat ingredients may be substituted, if desired.

After four years of baking with SPLENDA®, I can't imagine my life without it. My family and friends can't tell the difference.

Try these recipes and pamper yourself with splendid, almost guilt-free, desserts.

Jennifer Eloff

Nutrient Analysis

Nutrient analysis of the recipes was performed by Info Access (1988) Inc., D Mills, Ontario using the nutritional accounting component of the CBORD Mer Management System. The nutrient database was the 1991 Canadian Nutrient Fil supplemented when necessary with reviewed and documented data from reliabl sources.

The analysis was carried out using Imperial measures except when the practica recipe quantity was metric. When there was a choice of ingredients the calculation were based on the first ingredient listed. Optional ingredients were not included in the analysis.

Canadian Diabetes Association Food Choice Values

The Canadian Diabetes Association Food Choice Values contained on each page are part of the Good Health Eating Guide System, 1994. Each of the food choice groups in the Good Health Eating Guide; Starch Foods, Fruit and Vegetables, Milk, Sugars, Protein Foods, Fats & Oils and Extras have symbols which identify foods with similar nutrients.

People with diabetes who use the Good Health Eating Guide System and the Food Choice Symbols have an individualized meal plan which indicates how many "choices" to make from each group at meals and snacks. This system allows people with diabetes to "fit" many of the delicious desserts contained in this book into their meal plan. Examples of the food choice groups are shown below.

■ **Starch Foods**
1 slice bread
1/2 cup corn

▮ **Fruit & Vegetables**
1/2 grapefruit
1 cup tomatoes

◆ **Milk**
1/2 cup milk
1/2 cup plain yogurt

✳ **Sugars**
1 short licorice
2 teaspoons sugar

◗ **Protein Foods**
1 slice poultry
1 egg

▲ **Fats & Oils**
1 teaspoon oil
1 teaspoon margarine

++ **Extras**
yellow beans
green peppers

Helpful Hints

1. Buttermilk Alternative: You can make sour milk. Add 1 tbsp (25 mL) lemon juice or white vinegar to 1-cup (250 mL) measuring cup and fill with milk. Set aside at least 3 minutes before using.

2. Pies: Spraying the glass pie dish with nonstick cooking spray enables easier removal of slices. Short Crust, page 104, and Crunchy Almond Crust, page 66, are possible alternatives to graham crusts. Sometimes, when making the pies, not all the pastry will be used, but on the plus side the fat and calories will be lower than indicated.

3. Muffins and Loaves: The recipes may be doubled, if desired. Many of the baked goods usually freeze very well. Wrap in plastic wrap and then in foil. Unwrap and defrost in the microwave. Since sugar normally helps preserve baked goods, refrigeration after 1 or 2 days is preferable.

4. Cheesecakes: At first people might think that a low-fat cheesecake with no sugar added means they're in for a major disappointment. Not at all! The good news is that these elegant cheesecakes taste rich, sweet and satisfying, and no one is going to miss all those extra calories and fat (see comparison given on page 54).

(a) **Crusts:** For maximum flexibility in mixing and matching a preferred crust with a particular recipe, all the significant crusts have been assigned nutritional analyses as well as the Canadian Diabetes Association Food Choice Values and/or Symbols.
   The Short Crust, page 104, is an excellent crust for cheesecakes. It retains its firm texture quite nicely. It is, however, higher in fat than the graham crusts for cheesecakes. Low-fat cheesecakes have a tendency to leak moisture while baking and a soggy crust is often the result. For the graham crusts, adding egg white and baking the crust 10 minutes longer produces a crisper crust. To reduce the fat in these cheesecakes even more, it is possible to omit the crust. Instead, simply spray the pan with nonstick cooking spray and sprinkle with ⅓ cup (75 mL) graham crumbs or Grape-Nuts cereal crumbs sweetened with 2 tbsp (25 mL) SPLENDA® Granular.

(b) **Spray** the sides of the springform pan with nonstick cooking spray. If your springform pan bottom is old and showing some signs of damage or rust, place a sheet of waxed paper on it, replace the ring, and trim. This prevents discoloration of the crust. For a higher cheesecake, use a smaller springform pan.

(c) **Soften** 8 oz (250 g) light cream cheese in the microwave oven for 45 seconds.

(d) **Cracks:** To help prevent cracks from forming on the surface of cheesecakes, bake in a water bath (see page 53). Cheesecakes that do not require a topping are best baked in this manner. Another method is to place a pan of boiling water next to the cheesecake while it is baking. This method, although not quite as good as the first, also serves to increase the overall humidity in the oven. When the cheesecake has finished baking, turn off the oven and prop the oven door open slightly. Run a knife along the sides of the cheesecake and pan to release steam and to relieve the surface tension. Return the cheesecake to the cooler oven, close the oven door and allow to cool completely. Refrigerate several hours or overnight. Cheesecakes taste even better when allowed to mature in the refrigerator for at least 1 day, preferably more.

(e) For a *firmer cheesecake,* here are some ideas, some of which will require time.
    i) Use yogurt cheese (See Helpful Hint #5) instead of skim milk yogurt. At the very least, always pour off excess liquid before measuring the yogurt.
    ii) The flour added to the cheesecake may be increased by 2 tbsp (25 mL). Conversely, omitting the flour in the recipe altogether will produce a smoother, creamier, less firm result.
    iii) Cottage cheese or ricotta cheese may be strained and pressed through a sieve to remove whey.
    iv) Use higher fat ingredients, such as regular cream cheese instead of light cream cheese or regular sour cream instead of skim milk yogurt.

(f) **Bake** the cheesecake until the perimeter is firm and the center is still slightly soft. It will set further as it cools.

5. *How to make yogurt cheese:* When plain yogurt is drained of the excess liquid called whey, it becomes a product called yogurt cheese. Generally, 3 cups (750 mL) yogurt will yield about 1 cup (250 mL) yogurt cheese. Replacing yogurt with yogurt cheese in the cheesecake recipes will result in a firmer cheesecake. Yogurt cheese may also be used as a substitute for sour cream.

(a) **Long method** *(and the most effective):* Place a colander lined with coffee filter paper or a triple thickness of cheesecloth over a bowl. Pour the yogurt onto the lining, cover with plastic wrap and refrigerate overnight.

(b) **Quick method** *(if time is a factor):* Place the yogurt in a fine-mesh sieve over a bowl and drain for 30 minutes.

6. *Cakes:* A correct balance of ingredients, as well as the correct technique, is required to achieve excellent results. Fruit juice (unsweetened) helps the rising process. Total substitution with SPLENDA® Granular in angel food or pound cakes isn't advisable. Where cakes and icings have been evaluated separately, choose an icing and add the nutritional values together.

7. *Self-rising cake-and-pastry flour for cakes:* Available in most larger supermarkets, this flour is helpful in producing light-textured cakes. To convert ordinary cake-and-pastry flour to self-rising, use this recipe for equally good results: 1 cup

(250 mL) cake-and-pastry flour, 1½ tsp (7 mL) baking powder and ¼ tsp (1 mL) salt. I find that the salt may be omitted, if desired.

8. Jams: These taste very fruity. The Canadian Diabetes Association Food Choice Values and/or Symbols are the same for all the jams.

9. Oven temperature: Unfortunately, one cannot rely on an oven thermometer for accuracy, unless it has been specifically calibrated for accuracy by an electrician or unless an auxiliary thermometer is placed inside the oven as a backup. (My previous oven, I later discovered, was too hot.) Do not trust the indicator light either. It can sometimes take a further 10 minutes or more for the oven to reach the temperature indicated on the dial. Everyone's oven tends to be different. Therefore, I have endeavored wherever possible to provide indicators besides the baking times. The baking times will provide an excellent guideline, but as a rule, it is always wise to monitor your baking. Remember, do not open the oven door before the first 10 minutes have elapsed (with the exception of cookies or other baked goods requiring shorter baking times); otherwise, a draft could interfere with the rising process. Unless otherwise indicated, the middle shelf in the oven is used during baking. Position two racks to divide the oven evenly into thirds when it is necessary to bake on more than one shelf at a time, for example, in the case of cookies.

10. Ingredient Clarifications:

(a) **SPLENDA® Granular:** This sugar substitute is the common ingredient in every recipe in the book. It measures just like sugar, spoon-for-spoon and cup-for-cup. SPLENDA® Granular is sold in supermarkets and pharmacies.

(b) **Light cream cheese:** Philadelphia Light Cream Cheese is the brand used. A bonus for U.S. consumers is that the Philadelphia Light Cream Cheese sold in the U.S.A. is apparently lower in fat than the Canadian equivalent.

(c) **Fructose:** This is a pure fruit sugar, naturally occurring in fruits and honey. It comes in granular form and is available in most larger supermarkets and in health food stores. With some SPLENDA® Granular desserts, there is a noticeable delay in the detection of sweetness and for that reason I occasionally include the use of small amounts of fructose. Studies with regard to people with diabetes have shown that it does not create the same roller-coaster result on the blood-glucose levels that sugar does.

(d) **Low-Calorie Dessert Topping Mix:** Weight Watchers brand.

(e) **All-fruit spreads:** These are made from fruit, with no added sugar.

(f) **Eggs:** Large eggs are used.

(g) **Fruit Pectin:** Slim Set brand.

(h) **Light Puddings:** Jell-O brand.

Smoothies, Shakes and Other Drinks

Strawberry Banana Smoothie

It tastes like a thick, rich ice cream shake, but is quite low in fat.

1½ cups	frozen, unsweetened strawberries	375 mL
1	banana, sliced	1
1 cup	skim milk yogurt	250 mL
¾ cup	SPLENDA® Granular	175 mL
½ cup	skim milk	125 mL

In blender, combine strawberries, banana, yogurt and SPLENDA® Granular; blend until smooth. Gradually blend in milk until desired consistency.
   Yield: 3½ cups (875 mL), 3 servings.

Variation:
Peach Banana Smoothie: Substitute frozen unsweetened peaches for the strawberries.

---

1 serving:
141 calories, 6.2 g protein, 0.4 g fat, 29.6 g carbohydrate, 1.8 g fiber
1½ 🖊 + 1 ◆ Skim + ½ ✳

Banana Lime Smoothie

Delicious and such a fun way for kids to load up on calcium and potassium!
Vary the amount of milk to control the thickness.

2 cups	sliced bananas	500 mL
1 cup	skim milk yogurt	250 mL
1 cup	SPLENDA® Granular	250 mL
⅓ cup	skim milk	75 mL
¼ cup	lime juice	50 mL
Dash	green food coloring	Dash

In plastic bag, freeze bananas overnight. In blender, combine bananas, yogurt, SPLENDA® Granular, milk, lime juice and green food coloring; blend until smooth.
   Yield: 3 cups (750 mL), 3 servings.

Variation:
Banana Orange Smoothie: Substitute ¼ cup (50 mL) frozen orange juice concentrate for the lime juice.

---

1 serving:
179 calories, 6.1 g protein, 0.7 g fat, 39.9 g carbohydrate, 1.8 g fiber
2½ 🍐 + 1 ◆ Skim + ½ ✳

Peach Smoothie

Ice cold, creamy and thick with an unbeatable peach flavor.

2 cups	Peach Sauce, page 114	500 mL
2 cups	skim milk yogurt	500 mL
¾ cup	SPLENDA® Granular	175 mL
¼ cup	skim milk	50 mL

In freezer container with lid, freeze Peach Sauce. In blender, combine frozen sauce, yogurt, SPLENDA® Granular and milk; blend until smooth.

Yield: 4 servings.

Variation:
Spiced Pear Smoothie: Substitute Spiced Pear Sauce, page 114, for the Peach Sauce.

---

1 serving:
139 calories, 7.3 g protein, 0.2 g fat, 27.8 g carbohydrate, 1.0 g fiber
1½ 🍎 + 1½ ◆ Skim + ½ ✳

Peachy Orange Banana Milkshake

So good — nutrition in a glass! (Pictured opposite page 28.)

1	can (14 oz/398 mL) unsweetened sliced peaches in pear juice OR 4 medium fresh peaches, sliced	1
1 cup	skim milk yogurt	250 mL
¾ cup	SPLENDA® Granular	175 mL
Half	can (12 oz/341 mL) frozen orange juice concentrate	Half
½ cup	skim milk	125 mL
1	banana	1
8	ice cubes	8

In blender, combine peaches, yogurt, SPLENDA® Granular, orange juice concentrate, milk and banana; blend until smooth. Add ice cubes; blend well again.

Yield: 6 cups (1.5 L), 6 servings.

Variations:

Peachy Orange Milkshake: Omit banana.

Orangy Apricot Banana Milkshake: Substitute canned unsweetened apricots or 5 large fresh apricots, sliced, for the peaches.

Orangy Apricot Milkshake: Omit banana.

---

1 serving:
143 calories, 4.2 g protein, 0.3 g fat, 32.6 g carbohydrate, 1.3 g fiber
2½ ◼ + ½ ◆ Skim + ½ ✳

Hot Chocolate Drink Mix

When I need a lift in the wintertime or after exercising in the cold outdoors, this is my favorite comfort beverage.

Dry Cocoa Mixture:

1½ cups	SPLENDA® Granular	375 mL
1 cup	skim milk powder	250 mL
⅓ cup	cocoa	75 mL

Chocolate Low-Calorie Dessert Topping (optional):

2 cups	prepared low-calorie dessert topping (see page 5)	500 mL
¼ cup	SPLENDA® Granular	50 mL
1 tbsp	cocoa	15 mL

Dry Cocoa Mixture: In container with lid, shake together SPLENDA® Granular, skim milk powder and cocoa to mix well. Store at room temperature.
Yield: Enough for 12 servings.

---

1 serving:
40 calories, 2.4 g protein, 0.6 g fat, 7.1 g carbohydrate, 0.9 g fiber
½ ◆ Skim + ½ ✳

Chocolate Low-Calorie Dessert Topping: Prepare dessert topping with skim milk as directed on package. Beat in SPLENDA® Granular and cocoa.
Yield: 8 servings.

To make 1 cup (250 mL) drink: Place 3 tbsp (45 mL) Drink Mix in coffee cup. Stir in just enough milk to form smooth paste. While stirring, fill with hot milk or boiling water. Garnish with generous scoop of Chocolate Low-Calorie Dessert Topping, if desired. Refrigerate the remaining topping.

---

1 serving with topping:
155 calories, 11.6 g protein, 2.8 g fat, 22.2 g carbohydrate, 1.1 g fiber
3 ◆ Skim + ½ ✳ + ½ ▲

Fruit Cup Cooler

Bursting with refreshing ice-cold fruit flavor. Garnish with sliced pineapple or oranges, if desired.

4 cups	unsweetened pineapple juice, chilled	1 L
2 cups	Peach Sauce, page 114	500 mL
1 cup	fresh orange juice	250 mL
¼ cup	SPLENDA® Granular	50 mL
1 tbsp	lemon juice	15 mL

In large bowl, combine pineapple juice, Peach Sauce, orange juice, SPLENDA® Granular and lemon juice; stir well. Chill in refrigerator (or freezer, to save time). Serve over crushed ice in tall glass.

Yield: 7 cups (1.75 L), 7 servings.

---

1 serving:
130 calories, 1.1 g protein, 0.2 g fat, 32.2 g carbohydrate, 0.8 g fiber
3 🖊

Pineapple Coconut Cocktail

These wonderful economical drinks were developed by my husband, Ian.

4 cups	unsweetened pineapple juice	1 L
1⅓ cups	SPLENDA® Granular	325 mL
4 cups	cold water	1 L
2 tsp	coconut extract	10 mL
2 tbsp	lemon juice (optional)	25 mL

Into each of two 4-cup (1 L) containers, pour half the pineapple juice. Stir half the SPLENDA® Granular into each container; top with half the water. Add half the coconut extract to each; stir well and chill. If desired, for zestier flavor, add half the lemon juice to each.

Yield: 8 cups (2 L), 8 servings.

Variations:
Piña Colada Mocktail: Add 1 tsp (5 mL) rum extract.

Grapefruit juice or any other unsweetened fruit juice: Omit coconut extract.

---

1 serving:
90 calories, 0.4 g protein, 0.1 g fat, 21.5 g carbohydrate, 0.1 g fiber
1½ 🔳 + ½ ✳️

Fruit Punch

Surprise your guests with this wonderful punch. Refrigerate whatever's left in a container with an airtight lid. It will still taste wonderful the next day.

1	pkg (20 oz/600 g) frozen unsweetened strawberries	1
4 cups	unsweetened pineapple juice, chilled	1 L
1	can (341 mL) frozen unsweetened apple juice concentrate, thawed	1
1⅔ cups	SPLENDA® Granular	400 mL
5 cups	carbonated salt-free water, chilled	1.25 L

In blender, purée, in batches, frozen strawberries with 2 cups (500 mL) of pineapple juice. Pour into large punch bowl. Add remaining pineapple juice and the apple juice concentrate. Stir in SPLENDA® Granular.

Add carbonated water carefully, stirring gently and briefly. (Do not worry about any froth accumulating on top as it will settle very soon.)

Yield: 13 cups (3.25 L), 13 servings.

---

1 serving:
122 calories, 0.6 g protein, 0.2 g fat, 30.4 g carbohydrate, 0.8 g fiber
2½ 🍏 + ½ ✳

Muffins, Buns and Sweet Breads

Black Forest Deluxe Muffins   16

Large Cranberry Orange Muffins   17

Applesauce Carrot Muffins   18

Cinnamon Buns   19

Koe(k)sisters   20

Spiced Apple Date Loaf   21

Pineapple Coconut Loaf   22

Glazed Lemon Loaf   23

Sun-Kissed Banana Bread   24

Banana Crêpes with Banana Rum Sauce   25

Dessert Crêpes with Orange Sauce   26

Black Forest Deluxe Muffins

These moist, jumbo muffins are more like cupcakes. (Pictured opposite page 28.)

2¼ cups	all-purpose flour	550 mL
1 cup	SPLENDA® Granular	250 mL
¾ cup	cocoa	175 mL
2 tbsp	baking powder	25 mL
¼ tsp	salt	1 mL
¼ tsp	cinnamon	1 mL
1	can (14 oz/398 mL) cherries in light syrup, drained	1
1	egg	1
1	egg white	1
1¾ cups	skim milk	425 mL
¼ cup	vegetable oil	50 mL
Coconut Topping:		
½ cup	finely flaked unsweetened coconut	125 mL
2 tbsp	SPLENDA® Granular	25 mL
1 tbsp	skim milk	15 mL

In large bowl, combine flour, SPLENDA® Granular, cocoa, baking powder, salt and cinnamon. Pit cherries and halve; stir into dry ingredients. Make well in center.

In separate bowl, beat egg with egg white with fork; stir in milk and oil. Pour into well and stir just until moistened. Fill 12 muffin cups full.

Coconut Topping: In small bowl, stir together coconut, SPLENDA® Granular and milk. Squeeze small amounts into loosely formed balls; gently push onto center of each muffin. Bake in 375°F (190°C) oven for 20 minutes or until tester comes out clean.

Yield: 12 large muffins.

---

1 muffin:
219 calories, 6.0 g protein, 9.1 g fat, 31.3 g carbohydrate, 3.2 g fiber
1 ◼ + ½ ◢ + 1 ✳ + ½ ◐ + 1½ ▲

Large Cranberry Orange Muffins

These showy muffins are extra special served with orange cream.

3 cups	all-purpose flour	750 mL
1½ cups	SPLENDA® Granular	375 mL
¼ cup	finely grated orange rind	50 mL
2 tbsp	baking powder	25 mL
½ tsp	salt	2 mL
2 cups	frozen unsweetened cranberries	500 mL
1	egg	1
1	egg white	1
1¾ cups	orange juice	425 mL
¼ cup	vegetable oil	50 mL

Spreadable Orange Cream:

½ cup	spreadable light cream cheese	125 mL
¼ cup	SPLENDA® Granular	50 mL
2 tbsp	frozen orange juice concentrate, thawed	25 mL
1 tsp	finely grated orange rind	5 mL

In large bowl, stir together flour, SPLENDA® Granular, orange rind, baking powder and salt. Chop cranberries in food processor with sharp blade; stir into dry ingredients.

In a separate bowl, beat egg with egg white with fork; stir in the orange juice and oil. Add to dry ingredients; stir just until moistened.

Fill 12 muffin cups full. Bake in 375°F (190°C) oven for about 25 minutes or until browning slightly. Cool 5 minutes in pan; remove and allow to cool on wire rack.

Spreadable Orange Cream*: Meanwhile, in bowl, beat together cream cheese, SPLENDA® Granular, orange juice concentrate and orange rind. Cut muffins in half; spread with orange cream.

Yield: 12 large muffins.

---

1 muffin:
229 calories, 5.5 g protein, 7.0 g fat, 35.9 g carbohydrate, 2.0 g fiber
1½ ■ + ½ ◩ + ½ ✳ + 1½ ▲

Applesauce Carrot Muffins

The idea for these muffins came from my cousin Leigh-Ann Taylor,
a teacher, who gave me a copy of her school's cookbook.

2 cups	all-purpose flour	500 mL
¾ cup	SPLENDA® Granular	175 mL
1 tbsp	baking powder	15 mL
1 tsp	cinnamon	5 mL
½ tsp	salt	2 mL
1 cup	finely grated carrot	250 mL
¼ cup	chopped walnuts	50 mL
1	egg	1
1	egg white	1
1½ cups	unsweetened applesauce	375 mL
3 tbsp	vegetable oil	45 mL

In large bowl, combine flour, SPLENDA® Granular, baking powder, cinnamon and salt; stir in carrot and walnuts.

In separate bowl, beat egg with egg white lightly with fork; stir in applesauce and oil. Add to dry ingredients; stir just until moistened.

Fill 12 muffin cups. Bake in 350°F (180°C) oven for 20 to 25 minutes or until lightly browned.

Yield: 12 muffins.

Variation:
Good Morning Muffins: For an entirely different twist, add ½ cup (125 mL) unsweetened desiccated coconut and ⅓ cup (75 mL) raisins; increase applesauce to 1¾ cups (425 mL). Bake 25 to 30 minutes.

---

1 Applesauce Carrot Muffin:
155 calories, 3.5 g protein, 5.7 g fat, 22.8 g carbohydrate, 1.5 g fiber
1 ▇ + ½ ◢ + 1 ▲

1 Good Morning Muffin:
196 calories, 3.9 g protein, 8.1 g fat, 27.9 g carbohydrate, 1.9 g fiber
1 ▇ + 1 ◢ + 1½ ▲

Cinnamon Buns

These super cinnamon buns will impress your family and friends.

1 lb	frozen white bread dough	500 g

Filling:

	Cinnamon Butter, page 117	

Cream Cheese Icing:

½ cup	low-fat cottage cheese	125 mL
½ cup	light cream cheese, softened (see page 5)	125 mL
⅓ cup	SPLENDA® Granular	75 mL
2 tbsp	diet margarine	25 mL
1 tsp	vanilla extract	5 mL

Place dough in greased loaf pan and cover with plastic wrap to prevent drying out. Allow to thaw and rise according to directions on package. Roll out with heavy rolling pin to 12 x 15-inch (30 x 38 cm) rectangle. If dough resists being rolled, cover with towel and allow to rest for 5 minutes.

Filling: Spread dough with Cinnamon Butter, leaving ½-inch (1 cm) border free. Starting at one long side, roll up tightly, jelly-roll style; pinch seam to seal. Cut crosswise in 12 pieces (or 9 pieces for larger cinnamon buns).

Arrange cut sides down in 2 greased 8-inch (1.2 L) round cake pans. (Packing them closely will allow higher rising. One pan will then have fewer buns; place something ovenproof, such as balls made from aluminum foil, up against them to get same effect. Alternatively place all in one pan for pull-apart style buns.) Cover with plastic wrap and damp towel. Place in oven preheated to 200°F/100°C (and then switched off) for 45 minutes or until doubled in size. Bake in 350°F (180°C) oven for 25 minutes.

Cream Cheese Icing: In food processor or blender, process cottage cheese until smooth. Add cream cheese, SPLENDA® Granular, margarine and vanilla; process until smooth. Spread over warm buns.

Yield: 12 buns.

---

1 bun:

201 calories, 5.1 g protein, 10.3 g fat, 21.9 g carbohydrate, 0.1 g fiber

1 ▪ + ½ ✳ + ½ ◢ + 1½ ▲

19

Koe(k)sisters

A traditional favorite in South Africa originating from the Malay people. Best the first day. Store in a covered casserole dish. Do be careful of the hot oil. (Pictured opposite page 28.)

2½ cups	Vanilla- or Maple-Flavored Syrup, page 116, cooled	625 mL
Soft Dough:		
4 cups	all-purpose flour	1 L
4 tsp	baking powder	20 mL
½ tsp	salt	2 mL
2 tbsp	butter or margarine	25 mL
1	egg, lightly beaten	1
1⅔ cups	skim milk	400 mL
	Vegetable oil for deep frying	

Refrigerate Vanilla-Flavored Syrup for about 1 hour. Just before using, place in saucepan in large basin filled with ice to keep from becoming too warm.

Soft dough: In large bowl, stir together flour, baking powder and salt; cut in butter with pastry blender. Add egg, then milk, stirring gradually just until soft dough forms. Knead well, then refrigerate for 2 hours or longer.

Divide dough into 3 portions. Roll out each to ¼-inch (5 mm) thickness; cut into long ½-inch (1 cm) wide strips. Using 3 strips each, plait (braid) strips. Cut into 2 to 2½-inch (5 to 6 cm) lengths, pinching both ends tightly.

In deep-fat fryer, heat oil to 370°F (185°C); fry 5 or 6 koe(k)sisters at a time for 1 to 2 minutes or until light brown underneath. Flip with fork; fry to golden brown on other side.

Remove with lifter and drain briefly on absorbent paper; plunge into cold Vanilla-Flavored Syrup. Remove from syrup, allowing excess to drip back into syrup. Place on flat baking pan to drain slightly.

Yield: 7 dozen, 2 koe(k)sisters per serving.

---

2 koe(k)sisters:
118 calories, 1.8 g protein, 5.8 g fat, 14.4 g carbohydrate, 0.4 g fiber
1 ■ + 1 ▲

Spiced Apple Date Loaf

A flavorful loaf — the addition of dates makes it really lovely. Serve at room temperature, sliced and buttered, if desired.

2¼ cups	all-purpose flour	550 mL
1 cup	SPLENDA® Granular	250 mL
2 tsp	baking powder	10 mL
1 tsp	cinnamon	5 mL
½ tsp	baking soda	2 mL
½ tsp	ground ginger	2 mL
¼ tsp	ground nutmeg	1 mL
¼ tsp	ground cloves	1 mL
½ cup	chopped dates	125 mL
1	egg	1
1 cup	unsweetened apple juice	250 mL
½ cup	unsweetened applesauce	125 mL
¼ cup	vegetable oil	50 mL
1 tbsp	lemon juice	15 mL

In large bowl, stir together flour, SPLENDA® Granular, baking powder, cinnamon, baking soda, ginger, nutmeg and cloves. Stir in dates. Make well in center.

In small bowl, beat egg lightly with fork. Stir in apple juice, applesauce, oil and lemon juice. Pour into well; stir just until moistened.

Scoop evenly into lightly greased 9 x 5 x 3-inch (2 L) loaf pan. Bake in 350°F (180°C) oven for 40 to 45 minutes or until golden brown. Run knife along sides of loaf. Remove to cake rack and let cool. Store in sealed plastic bread bag at room temperature. Refrigerate after 2 days to prolong freshness.

Yield: 1 loaf, 16 servings.

---

1 serving:
132 calories, 2.4 g protein, 4.0 g fat, 22.1 g carbohydrate, 1.2 g fiber
1 ▣ + ½ ◪ + 1 ▲

Pineapple Coconut Loaf

Makes two flavorful, moist loaves. Freeze the extra loaf, if desired.
A taste of the Caribbean!

4 cups	all-purpose flour	1 L
2 tbsp	baking powder	25 mL
1 tsp	salt	5 mL
1 cup	finely flaked unsweetened coconut	250 mL
¼ cup	butter or margarine, softened	50 mL
2	eggs	2
2 cups	SPLENDA® Granular	500 mL
2 cups	skim milk	500 mL
1	can (14 oz/398 mL) unsweetened crushed pineapple, undrained	1
4 tsp	coconut extract	20 mL

In large bowl, combine flour, baking powder and salt; stir in coconut.

In separate bowl, beat together butter, eggs and SPLENDA® Granular. Stir in milk, pineapple and coconut extract, beating briefly to mix well. Add to dry ingredients, stirring just until moistened.

Pour into 2 lightly greased 9 x 5 x 3-inch (2 L) loaf pans. Bake in 350°F (180°C) oven for 45 minutes or until tester inserted in center comes out clean. If loaves brown too quickly, cover lightly with foil.

Yield: 2 loaves, 32 servings.

---

1 serving:
115 calories, 2.8 g protein, 3.8 g fat, 17.4 g carbohydrate, 0.7 g fiber
1 ▣ + ½ ▲ + 1 ⊞

Glazed Lemon Loaf

A wonderful loaf with a tender texture and a tangy glaze.

2 cups	all-purpose flour	500 mL
1 cup	SPLENDA® Granular	250 mL
2 tsp	baking powder	10 mL
½ tsp	baking soda	2 mL
½ tsp	salt	2 mL
⅓ cup	butter or margarine	75 mL
2 tsp	finely grated lemon rind	10 mL
2	eggs, lightly beaten	2
1¼ cups	buttermilk (see page 3)	300 mL
Lemon Glaze:		
¼ cup	SPLENDA® Granular	50 mL
2 tbsp	lemon juice	25 mL
½ tsp	cornstarch	2 mL
Dash	yellow food coloring (optional)	Dash

In large bowl, combine flour, SPLENDA® Granular, baking powder, baking soda and salt; cut in butter with pastry blender. Stir in lemon rind.

Stir eggs into buttermilk; stir into dry ingredients just until moistened.

Spoon into lightly greased 9 x 5 x 3-inch (2 L) loaf pan. Bake in 350°F (180°C) oven for 25 minutes. Cover lightly with foil to prevent browning; bake for 15 minutes or until tester inserted in center comes out clean.

Lemon Glaze: Meanwhile, in small saucepan, combine SPLENDA® Granular, lemon juice and cornstarch; stir over high heat until boiling. Stir in food coloring. Allow to cool for a few minutes. Brush over warm loaf.

Yield: 1 loaf, 16 servings.

---

1 serving:
132 calories, 3.1 g protein, 4.8 g fat, 18.8 g carbohydrate, 0.6 g fiber
1 ▣ + ½ ✳ + 1 ▲

Sun-Kissed Banana Bread

A delightful variation of an old favorite. For special occasions, serve with Spreadable Orange Cream, page 17.

1¼ cups	all-purpose flour	300 mL
1 cup	whole wheat flour	250 mL
¾ cup	SPLENDA® Granular	175 mL
¼ cup	sunflower seeds	50 mL
2 tbsp	wheat germ	25 mL
1 tbsp	baking powder	15 mL
1	egg	1
2 tbsp	vegetable oil	25 mL
1¼ cups	mashed ripe banana	300 mL
¾ cup	orange juice	175 mL
1 tsp	vanilla extract	5 mL

In large bowl, combine all-purpose and whole wheat flours, SPLENDA® Granular, sunflower seeds, wheat germ and baking powder. In separate bowl, beat egg with oil; beat in banana until blended. Stir in orange juice and vanilla. Stir into dry ingredients just until moistened.

Scoop into lightly greased 9 x 5 x 3-inch (2 L) loaf pan. Bake in 350°F (180°C) oven for 45 to 50 minutes or until tester inserted in center comes out clean, covering loosely with foil during last 10 minutes to prevent overbrowning, if necessary.

Yield: 1 loaf, 16 servings.

---

1 serving:
125 calories, 3.4 g protein, 3.6 g fat, 20.7 g carbohydrate, 2.0 g fiber
1 ■ + ½ ◢ + ½ ▲

Banana Crêpes with Banana Rum Sauce

For another delicious dessert idea, serve the sauce over vanilla ice cream.

1½ cups	skim milk	375 mL
1	large ripe banana, mashed	1
2	eggs	2
2 tbsp	vegetable oil	25 mL
1 tsp	vanilla extract	5 mL
1¼ cups	all-purpose flour	300 mL
¼ cup	SPLENDA® Granular	50 mL
¼ tsp	salt	1 mL
½ tsp	butter	2 mL
Banana Rum Sauce:		
4	bananas, thickly sliced	4
1 tbsp	butter	15 mL
½ cup	unsweetened pineapple juice OR orange juice	125 mL
⅓ cup	SPLENDA® Granular	75 mL
1 tbsp	lemon juice	15 mL
2 tsp	cornstarch	10 mL
1 tsp	rum extract	5 mL

In blender, place milk, banana, eggs, oil, vanilla, flour, SPLENDA® Granular and salt; blend until smooth.

Melt butter in 5-inch (12 cm) crêpe pan until sizzling for first crêpe; thereafter use nonstick cooking spray. For each crêpe, drop 3 tbsp (45 mL) batter into pan, tilting to spread evenly. Cook for about 1 minute on each side or until golden. Keep warm.

Banana Rum Sauce: In skillet, fry bananas in butter for 1 minute. Add pineapple juice and SPLENDA® Granular. Stir lemon juice with cornstarch until a paste; stir into pan. Stir in rum extract; cook until thickened. Fold crêpes and serve with warm sauce.

Yield: Makes 18 crêpes.

---

2 crêpes:
213 calories, 5.3 g protein, 6.0 g fat, 35.3 g carbohydrate, 1.7 g fiber
1 ■ + 1½ ▰ + 1 ▲

Dessert Crêpes with Orange Sauce

This is my son Daniel's favorite crêpe recipe.

1¼ cups	2% milk	300 mL
1 cup	cake-and-pastry flour	250 mL
2	eggs	2
2 tbsp	SPLENDA® Granular	25 mL
1 tbsp	diet margarine	15 mL
½ tsp	orange extract	2 mL
½ tsp	salt	2 mL
Orange Sauce:		
2 tbsp	cornstarch	25 mL
1½ cups	orange juice	375 mL
¾ cup	SPLENDA® Granular	175 mL
⅛ tsp	salt	0.5 mL
1 tsp	each vegetable oil and lemon juice	5 mL
1 tsp	finely grated orange rind	5 mL
½ cup	spreadable light cream cheese	125 mL
1	can (10 oz/284 mL) mandarin orange segments	1

In blender, combine milk, flour, eggs, SPLENDA® Granular, margarine, orange extract and salt; blend until smooth, scraping down sides occasionally.

Spray 5-inch (12 cm) crêpe pan with nonstick cooking spray. For each crêpe, pour scant ¼ cup (50 mL) batter into pan; cook until bubbles form and top sets slightly. Flip and cook 1 minute longer. Keep warm.

Orange Sauce: In small saucepan, dissolve cornstarch in ¼ cup (50 mL) of the orange juice. Stir in remaining orange juice, SPLENDA® Granular and salt. Cook over medium heat until boiling and thickened. Remove from heat. Stir in oil, lemon juice and orange rind.

Assembly: Spread each crêpe with 2 tsp (10 mL) of cream cheese. Fold the crêpes and place in a shallow casserole dish. Pour the hot orange sauce over crêpes and garnish with mandarin orange segments.

Yield: 6 servings, 2 crêpes each.

---

2 crêpes:
249 calories, 8.0 g protein, 7.9 g fat, 36.5 g carbohydrate, 0.9 g fiber
1½ ■ + 1 ◪ + ½ ✳ + ½ ◉

Cakes and Coffee Cakes

Peach Melba Chiffon Cake   28

Lemon-and-Lime Chiffon Cake   29

Orange Chiffon Birthday Cake   30

Marble Chiffon Cake   31

Strawberry Shortcake   32

Pineapple Upside-Down Cake   33

White Buttermilk Cake   34

Double Chocolate Fudge Cake   35

Triple Lemon Cake Roll   36

Rhumba-ba   37

Rhubarb Coffee Cake   39

Glazed Apricot Coffee Cake   40

Peach Melba Chiffon Cake

A work of art and it tastes as good as it looks! (Pictured on cover.)

2¼ cups	self-rising cake-and-pastry flour	550 mL
1½ cups	SPLENDA® Granular	375 mL
1½ tsp	baking powder	7 mL
½ tsp	baking soda	2 mL
½ cup	vegetable oil	125 mL
3	egg yolks	3
1¼ cups	buttermilk (see page 3)	300 mL
1 tsp	vanilla extract	5 mL
7	egg whites	7
½ tsp	cream of tartar	2 mL
Peach Melba Glaze:		
½ cup	SPLENDA® Granular	125 mL
2 tbsp	cornstarch	25 mL
1¼ cups	unsweetened pineapple juice	300 mL
1 tbsp	lemon juice	15 mL
Dash	red food coloring	Dash
8	slices canned unsweetened peaches	8
18	fresh raspberries	18

In bowl, sift together first four ingredients; make well in center. To well, add oil, egg yolks, buttermilk and vanilla. Using wooden spoon, mix well.

In large bowl, beat egg whites and cream of tartar until stiff peaks form. Add batter and fold in with under-and-over motion until just blended.

Pour into ungreased 10-inch (4 L) nonstick tube pan. Bake in 350°F (180°C) oven for 40 minutes or until top springs back when lightly touched. Invert pan onto wire rack (cake should release) and allow to cool.

Peach Melba Glaze: In saucepan, combine SPLENDA® Granular, cornstarch and pineapple juice; cook, stirring over medium heat until boiling and thickened. Stir in lemon juice. Add enough red food coloring to make bright red.

Arrange peaches and raspberries on cake; pour glaze over top.

Yield: 16 servings.

---

1 serving:
180 calories, 4.6 g protein, 8.2 g fat, 21.8 g carbohydrate, 0.8 g fiber
1 ■ + ½ ◗ + 1½ ▲

Peachy Orange Banana Milkshake (p. 10), Koe(k)sisters (p. 20), and Black Forest Deluxe Muffins (p. 16)

Lemon-and-Lime Chiffon Cake

A little indulgent, but birthdays come but once a year! Slice the cake in half horizontally and frost with Lemon Butter Icing, page 113, between the layers and on top.

2¼ cups	self-rising cake-and-pastry flour (see page 4)	550 mL
1½ cups	SPLENDA® Granular	375 mL
2 tsp	baking powder	10 mL
½ cup	vegetable oil	125 mL
3	egg yolks	3
⅔ cup	apple juice	150 mL
¼ cup	lemon juice	50 mL
2 tbsp	lime juice	25 mL
2 tsp	finely grated lime rind	10 mL
1 tsp	finely grated lemon rind	5 mL
7	egg whites	7
½ tsp	cream of tartar	2 mL
	Lemon Butter Icing, page 113	

In bowl, sift together flour, SPLENDA® Granular and baking powder; make well in center. To well, add oil, egg yolks, apple juice, lemon juice, lime juice, lime and lemon rinds. Using wooden spoon, beat until well combined.

In large bowl, beat egg whites and cream of tartar until stiff peaks form. Add batter and fold in with under-and-over motion until just blended.

Pour into ungreased 10-inch (4 L) nonstick tube pan. Bake in 350°F (180°C) oven for 40 minutes or until top springs back when lightly touched. Invert pan onto wire rack (cake should release) and allow to cool.

Yield: 16 servings.

Tip: For a less calorific solution, use diet margarine in the butter icing. Pour just enough icing over the cake to cover the top and drizzle down the sides.

---

1 serving with icing:
212 calories, 5.7 g protein, 10.8 g fat, 22.9 g carbohydrate, 0.6 g fiber
1 [■] + ½ [✱] + ½ [◑] + 2 [▲]

Orange Chiffon Birthday Cake

Very orangy flavor. Another idea is to cut the cake in half and frost with Orange Butter Icing (page 113) in the middle and on top.

2¼ cups	self-rising cake-and-pastry flour (see page 4)	550 mL
1¼ cups	SPLENDA® Granular	300 mL
2 tsp	baking powder	10 mL
½ cup	vegetable oil	125 mL
3	egg yolks	3
¾ cup	orange juice	175 mL
1 tbsp	lemon juice	15 mL
2 tbsp	finely grated orange rind	25 mL
7	egg whites	7
½ tsp	cream of tartar	2 mL
Orange Glaze:		
¾ cup	orange juice	175 mL
½ cup	SPLENDA® Granular	125 mL
4 tsp	cornstarch	20 mL
½ tsp	vegetable oil	2 mL
½ tsp	lemon juice	2 mL

In bowl, sift together flour, SPLENDA® Granular and baking powder; make well in center. To well, add oil, egg yolks, orange juice, lemon juice and orange rind. Using wooden spoon, beat until well combined.

In large bowl, beat egg whites and cream of tartar until stiff peaks form. Add batter and fold in with under-and-over motion until just blended.

Pour into ungreased 10-inch (25 cm) nonstick Bundt pan. Bake in 325°F (160°C) oven for 45 minutes or until top springs back when lightly touched. Invert pan onto wire rack (cake should release) and allow to cool.

Orange Glaze: In saucepan, combine orange juice, SPLENDA® Granular and cornstarch; cook, stirring, over medium heat until boiling and thickened. Stir in oil and lemon juice. Cool slightly. Pour over cake.

Yield: 16 servings.

---

1 serving:
168 calories, 4.0 g protein, 8.1 g fat, 19.4 g carbohydrate, 0.7 g fiber
1 ■ + ½ ◢ + 1½ ▲

Marble Chiffon Cake

The Chocolate Fudge Topping sets with a marvelous sheen.

Chocolate Batter:

⅓ cup	cocoa	75 mL
¼ cup	unsweetened apple juice	50 mL
3 tbsp	SPLENDA® Granular	45 mL
1 tbsp	vegetable oil	15 mL

Cake Batter:

2 cups	self-rising cake-and-pastry flour (see page 4)	500 mL
1¼ cups	SPLENDA® Granular	300 mL
2 tsp	baking powder	10 mL
1¼ cups	unsweetened apple juice	300 mL
½ cup	vegetable oil	125 mL
2 tsp	vanilla extract	10 mL
2	egg yolks	2
8	egg whites	8
½ tsp	cream of tartar	2 mL
	Chocolate Fudge Topping, page 111	

Chocolate Batter: In small bowl, stir together cocoa, apple juice, SPLENDA® Granular and oil. Set aside.

Cake Batter: In bowl, sift together flour, SPLENDA® Granular and baking powder. In small bowl, combine apple juice, oil and vanilla. In another bowl, beat egg yolks; alternately add dry ingredients and oil mixture, making 2 additions of each and beating on high speed for 2 minutes after each addition. In large bowl, beat egg whites with cream of tartar until stiff peaks form. Pour in batter in thin stream and fold in with under-and-over motion until just blended.

Remove one-third of the batter to small bowl; fold in chocolate mixture. Pour half the light batter into ungreased 10-inch (25 cm) nonstick Bundt pan. Top with half the chocolate batter. Repeat. With knife, swirl through layers gently to create marble pattern. Bake in 325°F (160°C) oven for 50 minutes or until top springs back when lightly touched. Invert pan onto wire rack and allow to cool. Pour Chocolate Fudge Topping over top and allow it to drizzle down sides.

Yield: 16 servings.

---

1 serving:
198 calories, 4.9 g protein, 10.3 g fat, 22.6 g carbohydrate, 2.1 g fiber
1 ▣ + ½ ✳ + ½ ◐ + 1½ ▲

Strawberry Shortcake

An old favorite. Try this easy method using your food processor. (Pictured opposite page 29.)

20	large strawberries, sliced	20
3 tbsp	SPLENDA® Granular	45 mL
Shortcake:		
2 cups	all-purpose flour	500 mL
⅓ cup	SPLENDA® Granular	75 mL
1 tbsp	baking powder	15 mL
¼ tsp	salt	1 mL
¼ cup	butter or margarine	50 mL
¾ cup	buttermilk (see page 3)	175 mL
1	egg white, lightly beaten	1
	Strawberry Whipped Topping, page 111	

Toss strawberries with SPLENDA® Granular. Set aside.

Shortcake: In bowl, combine flour, SPLENDA® Granular, baking powder and salt; cut in butter until mixture is crumbly in texture.

In food processor with dough blade, process buttermilk and egg white together. Add flour mixture; process on medium-low speed until sticky ball forms.

On lightly floured surface, pat dough to about ¾-inch (2 cm) thickness. Using 2½-inch (6 cm) round cookie cutter or glass, cut out 7 rounds. Gather remaining dough into ball and again pat to ¾-inch (2 cm) thickness. Cut out 3 more rounds. Place on greased baking sheet. Bake in 450°F (230°C) oven for 12 to 14 minutes or until light golden brown. Cool on wire rack.

Split biscuits in half; spread with Strawberry Whipped Topping. Place 2 sliced strawberries on each biscuit. Serve immediately.

Yield: 10 servings.

---

1 serving:
188 calories, 4.6 g protein, 6.5 g fat, 28.3 g carbohydrate, 1.9 g fiber
1 ■ + ½ ▨ + ½ ✱ + 1½ ▲

Pineapple Upside-Down Cake

A slightly different twist on an old favorite. (Pictured opposite page 29.)

Pineapple Topping:

1 tbsp	butter, melted	15 mL
¼ tsp	maple extract	1 mL
¼ cup	SPLENDA® Granular	50 mL
5½	slices drained canned unsweetened pineapple, reserving 1 tbsp (15 mL) juice	5½
10	fresh or frozen cranberries	10

Cake:

¼ cup	butter or margarine, softened	50 mL
1	egg	1
½ tsp	maple extract	2 mL
1½ cups	all-purpose flour	375 mL
⅔ cup	SPLENDA® Granular	150 mL
2 tsp	baking powder	10 mL
¼ tsp	salt	1 mL
¾ cup	skim milk	175 mL

Pineapple Topping: Spread butter evenly in 9-inch (1.5 L) round cake pan. Sprinkle with maple extract, mixing evenly with pastry brush. Sprinkle with SPLENDA® Granular. Drizzle pineapple juice over top. Halve all but 1 of the pineapple slices; place around perimeter of pan. Place whole slice in centre. Position 1 cranberry in center of each slice.

Cake: In bowl, beat together butter, egg and maple extract. In separate bowl, sift together flour, SPLENDA® Granular, baking powder and salt; add half to egg mixture along with half of the milk. Beat. Add remaining dry ingredients and milk; beat until smooth. Spread evenly over fruit, smoothing with back of spoon. Bake in 350°F (180°C) oven for 30 to 35 minutes or until slightly browned. Invert immediately onto cake plate. Serve warm or at room temperature.

Yield: 8 servings.

---

1 serving:

192 calories, 4.1 g protein, 8.0 g fat, 25.6 g carbohydrate, 1.0 g fiber

1 ■ + ½ ◢ + ½ ✳ + 1½ ▲

White Buttermilk Cake

A delicately textured cake. Frost with any of the Creamy Butter Icings,
page 113. See cakes, page 4.

½ cup	shortening	125 mL
4	egg whites	4
1 tsp	vanilla extract	5 mL
2½ cups	cake-and-pastry flour	625 mL
2 cups	SPLENDA® Granular	500 mL
6 tsp	baking powder	30 mL
½ tsp	baking soda	2 mL
1⅓ cups	buttermilk (see page 3)	325 mL

In large bowl, beat shortening until softened; beat in egg whites and vanilla until smooth. In separate bowl, sift together flour, SPLENDA® Granular, baking powder and baking soda; add to egg mixture alternately with buttermilk, making 2 additions of dry and 1 of buttermilk and beating 30 seconds to 1 minute after each addition until smooth.

Divide batter between 2 greased 8-inch (1.2 L) round cake pans, smoothing lightly with back of spoon. Bake in 350°F (180°C) oven for 30 to 35 minutes or until cake tester inserted in center comes out clean.

Invert gently onto wire racks and allow to cool thoroughly before frosting. Cover cake and leave outside fridge no longer than 2 days.

Yield: 12 servings.

---

1 serving without icing:
201 calories, 4.6 g protein, 8.7 g fat, 25.1 g carbohydrate, 0.8 g fiber
1½ ▣ + 1½ ▲ + 1 ✚

Double Chocolate Fudge Cake

A moist layer cake with a rich, sweet chocolate frosting. Self-rising cake-and-pastry flour is found in most larger supermarkets. To convert regular cake-and-pastry flour to self-rising, see Helpful Hints, page 4.

½ cup	shortening	125 mL
2	eggs	2
2¼ cups	self-rising cake-and-pastry flour (see page 4)	550 mL
1¾ cups	SPLENDA® Granular	425 mL
½ cup	cocoa	125 mL
2 tsp	baking powder	10 mL
½ tsp	baking soda	2 mL
1¼ cups	buttermilk (see page 3)	300 mL
⅔ cup	unsweetened apple juice	150 mL
	Chocolate Frosting, page 112 or Chocolate Butter Icing, page 113 (see cakes, page 4)	

In bowl, cream shortening. Add eggs and beat well. In separate bowl, sift together flour, SPLENDA® Granular, cocoa, baking powder and baking soda; add to egg mixture alternately with buttermilk and apple juice, making 2 additions of dry and 1 of buttermilk and apple juice and beating 30 seconds to 1 minute after each addition until smooth.

Divide batter between 2 greased 8-inch (1.2 L) round cake pans, smoothing lightly with back of spoon. Bake in 350°F (180°C) oven for 30 to 35 minutes or until cake tester inserted in center comes out clean.

Invert gently onto wire racks and allow to cool thoroughly before frosting with Chocolate Frosting or Chocolate Butter Icing. Serve same day or cover and refrigerate. Allow to stand at room temperature for 2 hours before serving.

Yield: 12 servings.

Variation:
Cupcakes: Fill 12 muffin cups full or 18 muffin cups half full. Bake for 20 to 25 minutes.

---

1 serving without icing:
213 calories, 4.9 g protein, 10.4 g fat, 25.8 g carbohydrate, 2.0 g fiber
1½ ■ + 2 ▲ + 1 ✛✛

Triple Lemon Cake Roll

A moist, dense roll with lemon in the cake, a lemon cheese filling and tangy lemon syrup drizzled on top.

1 cup	all-purpose flour	250 mL
1 tsp	baking powder	5 mL
2	egg yolks	2
½ cup	SPLENDA® Granular	125 mL
½ cup	unsweetened applesauce	125 mL
3 tbsp	buttermilk or soured milk (see page 3)	45 mL
1 tsp	vanilla extract	5 mL
1 tsp	grated lemon rind	5 mL
4	egg whites	4
¼ tsp	cream of tartar	1 mL
Lemon Cheese Filling:		
1 cup	low-fat cottage cheese	250 mL
4 oz	light cream cheese, softened (see page 5)	125 g
½ cup	SPLENDA® Granular	125 mL
2 tbsp	lemon juice	25 mL
2 tsp	grated lemon rind	10 mL
3	drops yellow food coloring	3
Lemon Syrup:		
2 tbsp	lemon juice	25 mL
½ tsp	cornstarch	2 mL
¼ cup	SPLENDA® Granular	50 mL
1	drop yellow food coloring	1

Spray 15 x 10-inch (38 x 25 cm) jelly-roll pan with nonstick cooking spray. Line pan with waxed paper; spray paper with nonstick cooking spray. Set aside.

In small bowl, combine flour and baking powder. In large bowl, beat egg yolks well; beat in SPLENDA® Granular, applesauce, buttermilk, vanilla and lemon rind. Add flour mixture; beat on low speed just until combined. In another bowl, beat egg whites with cream of tartar until very stiff peaks form; stir half into batter. Fold in remaining egg whites.

Spread batter evenly in jelly-roll pan. Bake in 375°F (190°C) oven for 12 to 15 minutes or until cake springs back when lightly touched in center. Loosen edges of cake from pan; invert onto clean towel. Remove paper; trim any brown crusty edges. Roll up towel and cake together; place seam side down on wire rack. Set aside to cool completely.

Lemon Cheese Filling: In food processor or blender with sharp blade, process cottage cheese until smooth. Add cream cheese, SPLENDA® Granular, lemon juice, lemon rind and food coloring; process until smooth.

Lemon Syrup: In small saucepan, stir lemon juice with cornstarch until smooth. Stir in SPLENDA® Granular and bring to boil, stirring. Remove from heat; stir in yellow food coloring.

Assembly: Unroll cake and spread with Lemon Cheese Filling, leaving ¼-inch (5 mm) border. Roll up gently from one short side without towel. Using soft pastry brush, brush lemon syrup over jelly-roll. Refrigerate.

Yield: 10 servings.

---

1 serving:

137 calories, 7.6 g protein, 4.3 g fat, 16.5 g carbohydrate, 0.7 g fiber

1 ▣ + 1 ◪

Rhumba-ba

This is an attractive dark-colored dessert, soaked in rum-flavored syrup and covered in an apricot glaze. Serve with ice cream if desired. Grape-Nuts cereal has no added sugar. Graham crumbs may be substituted; reduce SPLENDA® Granular to ½ cup (125 mL).

½ cup	warm water	125 mL
1 tsp	granulated fructose (see Helpful Hints, page 5)	5 mL
1 tbsp	active dry yeast	15 mL
¾ cup	Grape-Nuts cereal	175 mL
1¼ cups	all-purpose flour	300 mL
1 cup	SPLENDA® Granular	250 mL
½ tsp	salt	2 mL
2	eggs	2
2	egg whites	2
½ cup	raisins	125 mL
½ cup	butter or margarine, melted	125 mL
¼ cup	Grape-Nuts cereal, finely ground	50 mL

Rum-Flavored Syrup:

1¾ cups	SPLENDA® Granular	425 mL
1 cup	water	250 mL
¼ cup	granulated fructose (see page 5)	50 mL
1 tbsp	cornstarch	15 mL
1 tbsp	butter or margarine	15 mL
⅛ tsp	salt	0.5 mL
1 tbsp	rum extract (or to taste)	15 mL

Apricot Glaze:

½ cup	all-fruit apricot spread (see page 5)	125 mL
4 tsp	water	20 mL

In bowl with warm water, dissolve fructose. Add yeast; let stand 10 minutes or until frothy. Stir well.

In blender or food grinder, process ¾ cup (175 mL) Grape-Nuts cereal into fine crumbs; stir into yeast mixture. Stir in flour, SPLENDA® Granular, salt, eggs, egg whites and raisins. Beat about 3 minutes or until elastic and sticky. Cover and let rise in warm place until doubled, about 45 minutes. Stir down batter. Beat in butter for 2 minutes or until elastic and sticky.

Grease nonstick Bundt pan; dust with ground Grape-Nuts cereal. Spoon batter evenly into pan. Cover and let rise until doubled, about 45 minutes. Bake in 375°F (190°C) oven for 20 minutes or until well-browned and cake tester comes out clean. Turn out onto wire rack to cool slightly. Place on serving plate with substantial rim. Pierce all over top with fork.

Rum-Flavored Syrup: In saucepan, combine SPLENDA® Granular, water, fructose, cornstarch, butter and salt; bring to boil over medium heat. Remove from heat. Stir in rum extract. Slowly pour over cake. Do not remove excess that collects on plate. Let stand for 5 minutes.

Apricot Glaze: In small saucepan, heat apricot spread and water over medium heat until melted and very hot. Press through sieve. Spoon over cake, making sure all dry areas are covered, spooning from excess on plate. Serve at room temperature.

Yield: 16 servings.

---

1 serving:
189 calories, 3.7 g protein, 7.3 g fat, 27.4 g carbohydrate, 1.5 g fiber
1 ▣ + ½ ▰ + ½ ✳ + 1½ ▲

Rhubarb Coffee Cake

If you're a rhubarb lover, then you'll enjoy this cake smothered in Rhubarb
Sauce (page 115).

Fruit Filling:

2¼ cups	fresh or frozen cut-up rhubarb	550 mL
½ cup	SPLENDA® Granular	125 mL
⅓ cup	orange juice	75 mL
2 tbsp	cornstarch	25 mL

Cake:

1⅔ cups	all-purpose flour	400 mL
½ cup	SPLENDA® Granular	125 mL
1½ tsp	baking powder	7 mL
¼ tsp	baking soda	1 mL
2 tbsp	butter or margarine	25 mL
1	large egg white OR 1 small egg	1
1 cup	buttermilk OR soured milk (page 3)	250 mL
1 tsp	vanilla extract	5 mL

Topping:

⅓ cup	all-purpose flour	75 mL
2 tbsp	SPLENDA® Granular	25 mL
2 tbsp	diet margarine	25 mL

Fruit Filling: In saucepan, combine rhubarb, SPLENDA® Granular, orange juice
and cornstarch; bring to boil over medium heat, stirring. Reduce heat to minimum;
cover and simmer, stirring occasionally, about 10 minutes or until rhubarb is tender.

Cake: In bowl, combine flour, SPLENDA® Granular, baking powder and baking
soda; rub in butter with fingertips. In small bowl, beat egg white with fork until
frothy; stir in buttermilk and vanilla. Add to flour mixture and stir until moistened.
Spread half the batter evenly in lightly greased 8-inch (2 L) square cake pan.
Spread fruit filling over top. Drop remaining batter by large spoonfuls onto filling.

Topping: In small bowl, stir together flour and SPLENDA® Granular; stir in
margarine with fork until crumbly. Sprinkle mostly over areas not covered by batter.
Bake in 350°F (180°C) oven for 40 minutes or until browning in places.

Yield: 12 servings.

---

1 serving:
135 calories, 3.4 g protein, 3.3 g fat, 22.4 g carbohydrate, 1.1 g fiber
1 ▪ + ½ ✳ + ½ ▲

Glazed Apricot Coffee Cake

This cake has a dense but moist texture.

Apricot Purée:

1⅓ cups	dried apricots, cut in half	325 mL
¼ cup	SPLENDA® Granular	50 mL

Cake:

2¼ cups	self-rising cake-and-pastry flour (see page 4)	550 mL
1½ cups	SPLENDA® Granular	375 mL
2 tsp	baking powder	10 mL
½ cup	vegetable oil	125 mL
3	egg yolks	3
1 cup	water	250 mL
1 cup	apricot purée	250 mL
2 tsp	lemon juice	10 mL
7	egg whites, at room temperature	7
½ tsp	cream of tartar	2 mL

Apricot Glaze:

½ cup	all-fruit apricot spread (see page 5)	125 mL
4 tsp	water	20 mL

Apricot Purée: In saucepan, combine apricots, SPLENDA® Granular and enough water to cover; bring to boil over medium heat. Simmer, uncovered, until about ¼ cup (50 mL) liquid remains. Purée apricots and liquid in blender until smooth.

Cake: In large bowl, sift together flour, SPLENDA® Granular and baking powder; make well in center. To well add oil, egg yolks, water, apricot purée and lemon juice. Using wooden spoon, beat until well combined. In large bowl, beat egg whites and cream of tartar until stiff but not dry peaks form. Pour batter over egg whites in several additions, and fold in with wire whisk with under-and-over motion just until blended.

Pour into ungreased 10-inch (25 cm) nonstick Bundt pan. Bake in 325°F (160°C) oven for 55 to 60 minutes or until cake tester comes out clean, covering with foil after 30 minutes to prevent overbrowning. Invert pan onto wire rack and allow to cool. Remove cake from pan carefully and place on cake plate.

Apricot Glaze: In small saucepan, heat apricot spread and water over medium heat, stirring, until melted and very hot. Press through sieve. Spoon over cake.

Yield: 16 servings.

---

1 serving:
185 calories, 4.3 g protein, 8.0 g fat, 24.3 g carbohydrate, 1.6 g fiber
1 ■ + 1 ▰ + 1½ ▲

Cheesecakes

Graham Crumb Crust for Cheesecakes

This crust is baked extra long in order to better resist moisture leakage (see Helpful Hints, page 3). Low-fat cheesecakes have a tendency to leak moisture during baking.

¼ cup	Grape-Nuts cereal OR	50 mL
	graham crumbs	
½ cup	graham crumbs	125 mL
¼ cup	SPLENDA® Granular	50 mL
2 tbsp	diet margarine, melted	25 mL
1	egg white	1

In blender or small food grinder, blend Grape-Nuts cereal into fine crumbs; transfer to bowl. Stir in graham crumbs and SPLENDA® Granular; stir in margarine with fork.

In small bowl, beat egg white with fork until frothy; measure out 1 tbsp (15 mL) and stir into crumb mixture. Press onto bottom of 9-inch (2.5 L) springform pan. Bake in 350°F (180°C) oven for 15 to 20 minutes or until crisp. Be careful not to burn crust. Cool.

Yield: 1 nine-inch (23 cm) crust, 12 servings.

Variations:

Oreo Crumb Crust for Cheesecakes: Substitute Oreo crumbs for the graham crumbs. Add 1 tbsp (15 mL) cocoa and 1 extra tbsp (15 mL) SPLENDA® Granular.

Vanilla Crumb Crust for Cheesecakes: Substitute crushed vanilla wafers for graham cracker crumbs.

---

1 serving Graham Crumb Crust:
36 calories, 0.7 g protein, 1.4 g fat, 5.7 g carbohydrate, 0.4 g fiber
½ ✱ + ½ ▲

1 serving Oreo Crumb Crust:
40 calories, 0.7 g protein, 1.8 g fat, 5.7 g carbohydrate, 0.4 g fiber
½ ✱ + ½ ▲

1 serving Vanilla Crumb Crust:
35 calories, 0.5 g protein, 1.5 g fat, 5.1 g carbohydrate, 0.3 g fiber
½ ✱ + ½ ▲

No-Bake Strawberry Cheesecake

My favorite — pretty in pink with strawberries throughout. If calories are not a concern, garnish this cheesecake with low-calorie dessert topping and fresh strawberries. (Pictured opposite page 60.)

Vanilla Crumb Crust, page 42
OR Short Crust, page 104

Filling:

8 oz	light cream cheese, softened (see page 5)	250 g
¾ cup	SPLENDA® Granular	175 mL
1	envelope unflavored gelatin	1
¼ cup	cold water	50 mL
1	pkg (20 oz/600 g) frozen unsweetened strawberries, thawed	1
2 cups	prepared low-calorie dessert topping (see page 5)	500 mL

Bake Vanilla Crumb Crust as directed but in 8-inch (2 L) springform pan OR prepare Short Crust and bake for 15 minutes at 350°F (180°C).

Filling: In food processor or blender with sharp blade, process cream cheese with SPLENDA® Granular; set aside. In small saucepan, allow gelatin to soften in cold water; gently heat over low heat until dissolved.

Drain strawberries well, reserving juice. Add enough of the juice to gelatin to equal 1 cup (250 mL). Gradually add to cream cheese mixture; process until smooth. Fold in dessert topping. Stir in strawberries. Pour over cooled crust. Chill until set.

Yield: 12 servings.

---

1 serving:
128 calories, 3.3 g protein, 7.3 g fat, 13.0 g carbohydrate, 1.0 g fiber
½ ■ + ½ ✳ + 1½ ▲

Plain Cheesecake

This recipe is for the people who requested a plain cheesecake when they met me while promoting my first book. To further reduce the fat grams per serving, use the Graham Crumb Crust for Cheesecakes, page 42.

Short Crust, page 104

Batter:

2¼ cups	part-skim ricotta cheese	550 mL
8 oz	light cream cheese, softened (see page 5)	250 g
1¼ cups	SPLENDA® Granular	300 mL
1¼ cups	skim milk OR plain yogurt, drained	300 mL
2	eggs	2
¼ cup	all-purpose flour	50 mL
1 tsp	vanilla extract	5 mL
¼ tsp	salt	1 mL

Topping:

½ cup	light sour cream	125 mL
⅓ cup	skim milk yogurt	75 mL
⅓ cup	SPLENDA® Granular	75 mL

Prepare crust as directed on page 104. Press into a 9-inch (2.5 L) springform pan and bake at 350°F (180°C) for 15 minutes.

Batter: In food processor or blender with sharp blade, process ricotta cheese until smooth. Add cream cheese; process until smooth. Add SPLENDA® Granular, milk, eggs, flour, vanilla and salt; process on medium speed until smooth. Pour over cooled crust, smoothing surface with back of spoon. Bake in 350°F (180°C) oven for 40 minutes or until center is softly set.

Topping: In bowl, combine sour cream, yogurt and SPLENDA® Granular; beat with spoon until smooth. Spread over cheesecake. Bake a further 10 minutes. Refrigerate.

Yield: 12 servings.

---

1 serving:
253 calories, 11.7 g protein, 13.7 g fat, 20.3 g carbohydrate, 0.4 g fiber
½ ■ + 1 ◆ Skim + ½ ✳ + 1 ◑ + 2 ▲

Lemon Chiffon Cheesecake

This superb cheesecake has an airy, light texture with a refreshing tart flavor. For a really high cheesecake, use 2 cups (500 mL) cottage cheese, 3 eggs and a larger springform pan. Great with Short Crust.

Graham Crumb Crust for Cheesecakes,
page 42 OR Short Crust, page 104

Batter:

1 cup	2% cottage cheese	250 mL
8 oz	light cream cheese, softened (see page 5)	250 g
1¼ cups	SPLENDA® Granular	300 mL
¾ cup	skim milk yogurt	175 mL
2	egg yolks	2
¼ cup	lemon juice	50 mL
1 tbsp	finely grated lemon rind	15 mL
2	drops yellow food coloring	2
2	egg whites	2
⅛ tsp	cream of tartar	0.5 mL

Topping:

2 cups	prepared low-calorie dessert topping (see page 5)	500 mL
	Lemon slice	

Bake Graham Crumb Crust as directed but in 8-inch (2 L) springform pan OR prepare Short Crust and bake for 15 minutes at 350°F (180°C).

Batter: In food processor or blender with sharp blade, process cottage cheese until smooth. Add cream cheese; process until smooth. Add SPLENDA® Granular, yogurt, egg yolks, lemon juice, lemon rind and yellow food coloring; process until smooth.

In bowl, beat egg whites and cream of tartar until stiff peaks form; fold into cheese mixture until smooth. Pour over cooled crust. Bake in 350°F (180°C) oven for 35 to 40 minutes or until set and browning slightly. Let cool.

Topping: Spread topping over cooled cheesecake. Garnish with twisted lemon slice.

Yield: 12 servings.

---

1 serving:
154 calories, 7.3 g protein, 8.4 g fat, 12.8 g carbohydrate, 0.4 g fiber
½ ■ + ½ ✱ +1 ◑ + 1 ▲

Piña Colada Cheesecake

You'll receive raves for this cheesecake. Be sure to use unsweetened pineapple.

Vanilla Crumb Crust, page 42 OR
Short Crust, page 104

Batter:

2 cups	part-skim ricotta cheese	500 mL
8 oz	light cream cheese, softened	250 g
1 cup	SPLENDA® Granular	250 mL
½ cup	skim milk yogurt	125 mL
2	eggs	2
3 tbsp	all-purpose flour	45 mL
1 tsp	each coconut and rum extract	5 mL
1 cup	canned pineapple tidbits, drained	250 mL
5	maraschino cherries, finely chopped	5

Topping:

¼ cup	all-fruit apricot spread (see page 5)	50 mL
3	egg whites	3
¼ tsp	cream of tartar	1 mL
½ cup	canned pineapple tidbits, drained	125 mL
3	maraschino cherries, finely chopped	3

Bake Vanilla Crumb Crust as directed in 9-inch (2.5 L) springform pan OR prepare Short Crust and bake 15 minutes at 350°F (180°C).

Batter: In food processor or blender with sharp blade, process ricotta cheese until smooth. Add cream cheese, SPLENDA® Granular, yogurt, eggs, flour and coconut and rum extracts; process until smooth. Stir in pineapple, and cherries, if using. Pour over cooled crust. Bake in 350°F (180°C) oven for about 40 minutes or until just set in center. Let cool.

Topping: In blender, blend apricot spread until smooth. In bowl, beat egg whites with cream of tartar for 1 minute. Add apricot spread; beat at high speed until stiff peaks form. Spread over cooled cheesecake.

Dry pineapple tidbits with paper towel. Arrange over cheesecake along with cherries. Bake in 400°F (200°C) oven for 8 to 10 minutes or until slightly browned in places. Allow to cool completely at room temperature. Chill, uncovered.

Yield: 12 servings.

---

1 serving:
200 calories, 9.7 g protein, 9.2 g fat, 19.3 g carbohydrate, 0.7 g fiber
½ ■ + ½ ▰ + ½ ◆ Skim + ½ ✳ + 1 ▱ + 1 ▲

Cappuccino Cheesecake

The decorative topping enhances this flavorful cheesecake.

Oreo Crumb Crust, page 42

Batter:

2 cups	part-skim ricotta cheese	500 mL
8 oz	light cream cheese, softened	250 g
1½ cups	SPLENDA® Granular	375 mL
⅔ cup	skim milk yogurt	150 mL
2	eggs	2
1	egg white	1
¼ cup	all-purpose flour	50 mL
2 tbsp	instant coffee granules	25 mL
2 tbsp	hot water	25 mL
3 tbsp	cocoa	45 mL
¼ tsp	cinnamon	1 mL

Topping:

2 oz	light cream cheese, softened	60 g
⅔ cup	skim milk yogurt	150 mL
½ cup	SPLENDA® Granular	125 mL

Garnish:

3 tbsp	SPLENDA® Granular	45 mL
1 tbsp	cocoa	15 mL
⅛ tsp	cinnamon	0.5 mL

Prepare crust as directed.

Batter: In food processor or blender, process ricotta cheese until smooth. Add cream cheese; process until smooth. Add SPLENDA® Granular, yogurt, eggs, egg white and flour; process until smooth. Dissolve coffee in hot water. Add to batter along with cocoa and cinnamon; process until blended. Pour over cooled crust. Bake in 350°F (180°C) oven for 45 minutes or until center is just set. Let cool.

Topping: In food processor, process cream cheese. Add yogurt and SPLENDA® Granular; process until smooth. Spread over cooled cheesecake. Chill until set.

Garnish: Remove ring of pan. Place ½-inch (1 cm) wide strips of waxed paper across cheesecake, leaving space between each. In small bowl, stir together SPLENDA® Granular, cocoa and cinnamon; sift over top. Remove paper and chill. Refrigerate cheesecake.

Yield: 12 servings.

---

1 serving:
214 calories, 10.8 g protein, 11.0 g fat, 18.4 g carbohydrate, 1.2 g fiber
½ ■ + ½ ◆ Skim + ½ ✳ + 1 ◐ + 1½ ▲

Peanut Butter Chocolate Cheesecake

A rich combination of flavors reminiscent of Reese's Pieces.

Oreo Crumb Crust, page 42

Batter:

2 cups	low-fat ricotta cheese	500 mL
8 oz	light cream cheese, softened (see page 5)	250 g
1¼ cups	SPLENDA® Granular	300 mL
1 cup	skim milk yogurt	250 mL
2	eggs	2
⅓ cup	cocoa	75 mL
3 tbsp	peanut butter (no added salt or sugar)	45 mL

Peanut Whipped Topping:

2 cups	prepared low-calorie dessert topping (see page 5)	500 mL
⅓ cup	SPLENDA® Granular	75 mL
2 tsp	peanut butter	10 mL

Prepare crust as directed.

Batter: In food processor or blender with sharp blade, process ricotta cheese until very smooth. Add cream cheese; process until smooth. Add SPLENDA® Granular, yogurt, eggs, cocoa and peanut butter; process until smooth, scraping bowl occasionally. Pour over cooled crust. Bake in 350°F (180°C) oven for 45 to 50 minutes or until center is set. Let cool.

Peanut Whipped Topping: In bowl, beat together dessert topping, SPLENDA® Granular and peanut butter. Spread over cooled cheesecake. Refrigerate.

Yield: 12 servings.

---

1 serving:
227 calories, 11.2 g protein, 13.5 g fat, 16.9 g carbohydrate, 1.6 g fiber
½ ■ + ½ ◆ Skim + ½ ✳ + 1 ⦸ + 2 ▲

Chocolate Almond Cheesecake

This is one of my husband's favorite cheesecakes.

Oreo Crumb Crust, page 42, OR
Chocolate Single Pie Crust, page 56

Batter:

2 cups	part-skim ricotta cheese	500 mL
8 oz	light cream cheese, softened (see page 5)	250 g
1½ cups	SPLENDA® Granular	375 mL
1 cup	skim milk yogurt	250 mL
2	eggs	2
⅓ cup	cocoa	75 mL
2 tbsp	slivered almonds, finely ground	25 mL
½ oz	unsweetened or bittersweet chocolate, melted	15 g
½ tsp	almond extract	2 mL

Chocolate Whipped Topping:

2 cups	prepared low-calorie dessert topping (see page 5)	500 mL
⅓ cup	SPLENDA® Granular	75 mL
2 tbsp	cocoa	25 mL

Garnish:

2 tbsp	sliced blanched almonds	25 mL

Prepare crust as directed.

Batter: In food processor or blender with sharp blade, process ricotta cheese until smooth. Add cream cheese; process until smooth. Add SPLENDA® Granular, yogurt, eggs, cocoa, almonds, chocolate and almond extract; process until smooth. Pour over cooled crust. Bake in 350°F (180°C) oven for 45 to 50 minutes or until center is softly set. Let cool.

Chocolate Whipped Topping: In bowl, beat together dessert topping, SPLENDA® Granular and cocoa. Spread over cooled cheesecake. Garnish with almonds.

Yield: 12 servings.

---

1 serving:
224 calories, 10.8 g protein, 13.2 g fat, 17.6 g carbohydrate, 2.0 g fiber
½ ▪ + ½ ◆ Skim + ½ ✳ + 1 ◑ + 2 ▲

Chocolate Banana Cheesecake

A rich-tasting cheesecake, the color of milk chocolate.

Oreo Crumb Crust, page 42

Batter:

2 cups	part-skim ricotta cheese	500 mL
8 oz	light cream cheese, softened (see page 5)	250 g
1½ cups	SPLENDA® Granular	375 mL
1 cup	skim milk yogurt OR yogurt cheese (see page 4)	250 mL
2	eggs	2
2	bananas, mashed	2
⅓ cup	cocoa	75 mL
3 tbsp	all-purpose flour	45 mL
	Chocolate Whipped Topping, page 49, OR Chocolate Fudge Topping, page 111	

Prepare crust as directed.

Batter: In food processor or blender with sharp blade, process ricotta cheese until smooth. Add cream cheese; process until smooth. Add SPLENDA® Granular, yogurt, eggs, bananas, cocoa and flour; process until smooth, scraping down sides occasionally. Pour over cooled crust. Bake in 350°F (180°C) oven for 45 to 50 minutes or until center is just set. Let cool. Spread Chocolate Whipped Topping over cooled cheesecake. Refrigerate.

Yield: 12 servings.

---

1 serving:
234 calories, 10.8 g protein, 12.0 g fat, 23.0 g carbohydrate, 2.1 g fiber
½ ■ + ½ ● + ½ ◆ Skim + ½ ✳ + 1 ◐ + 2 ▲

Banana Custard Cheesecake

A *simply delightful cheesecake.*

Vanilla Crumb Crust, page 42 OR
Short Crust, page 104

Batter:

16 oz	light cream cheese, softened (see page 5)	500 g
1½ cups	SPLENDA® Granular	375 mL
1½ cups	mashed ripe banana	375 mL
1 cup	yogurt cheese (see page 4)	250 mL
3	eggs	3
⅓ cup	custard powder	75 mL
1 tbsp	vanilla extract	15 mL

Sweet Custard Topping:

½ cup	SPLENDA® Granular	125 mL
3 tbsp	custard powder	45 mL
1½ cups	skim milk	375 mL

Garnish:

1	large ripe banana, sliced	1
1 tbsp	lemon juice	15 mL

Bake Vanilla Crumb Crust as directed in 9-inch (2.5 L) springform pan OR prepare Short Crust and bake for 15 minutes at 350°F (180°C).

Batter: In food processor or blender with sharp blade, process cream cheese for 2 minutes. Add SPLENDA® Granular, banana, yogurt cheese, eggs, custard powder and vanilla; process until smooth. Pour over cooled crust. Bake in 350°F (180°C) oven for 50 minutes or until firm around edge and softly set in center. Let cool.

Sweet Custard Topping: In saucepan, combine SPLENDA® Granular and custard powder; gradually stir in milk and bring to boil over medium heat, stirring. Let cool slightly. Pour over cooled cheesecake. Cover surface with plastic wrap. Refrigerate.

Garnish: Just before serving, garnish with banana slices dipped in lemon juice.
Yield: 12 servings.

---

1 serving:
270 calories, 8.6 g protein, 13.6 g fat, 28.5 g carbohydrate, 1.0 g fiber
1 ■ + 1 ◢ + ½ ◆ Skim + ½ ◪ + 2½ ▲

Raisin-Studded Cheesecake

The Short Crust is perfect for any of the cheesecakes (see Helpful Hints, page 3).

Short Crust, page 104

Batter:

2⅓ cups	part-skim ricotta cheese	575 mL
8 oz	light cream cheese, softened (see page 5)	250 g
¾ cup	SPLENDA® Granular	175 mL
½ cup	skim evaporated milk	125 mL
2	egg yolks	2
2 tbsp	all-purpose flour	25 mL
2 tbsp	lemon juice	25 mL
2 tsp	vanilla extract	10 mL
¾ cup	seedless raisins	175 mL
2	egg whites	2
¼ tsp	cream of tartar	1 mL

Topping:

½ cup	light sour cream	125 mL
⅓ cup	skim milk yogurt	75 mL
⅓ cup	SPLENDA® Granular	75 mL

Prepare crust as directed. Press onto the bottom of a 9-inch (23 cm) springform pan. Bake in 350°F (180°C) oven for 15 minutes.

Batter: In food processor or blender with sharp blade, process ricotta cheese until smooth. Add cream cheese, SPLENDA® Granular, evaporated milk, egg yolks, flour, lemon juice and vanilla; process until smooth. Stir in raisins. In bowl, beat egg whites with cream of tartar until stiff peaks form; fold into batter. Pour over cooled crust. Bake in 350°F (180°C) oven for 40 minutes or until set.

Topping: In small bowl, stir together sour cream, yogurt and SPLENDA® Granular until smooth. Spread over top of cheesecake. Bake a further 10 minutes.

Yield: 12 servings.

---

1 serving:
286 calories, 11.6 g protein, 15.2 g fat, 26.1 g carbohydrate, 0.7 g fiber
½ ■ + 1 ◢ + 1 ◆ Skim + 1 ◙ + 2½ ▲

Strawberry Marble Cheesecake

This cheesecake is as pretty as a picture!

	Vanilla Crumb Crust, page 42	
Strawberry Topping:		
¼ cup	all-fruit strawberry spread (page 5)	50 mL
4 tsp	cornstarch	20 mL
4 tsp	water	20 mL
1¾ cups	halved frozen unsweetened strawberries	425 mL
2 tbsp	SPLENDA® Granular	25 mL
Batter:		
2¼ cups	part-skim ricotta cheese	550 mL
8 oz	light cream cheese, softened (see page 5)	250 g
1¼ cups	SPLENDA® Granular	300 mL
1¼ cups	plain yogurt	300 mL
2	eggs	2
¼ cup	all-purpose flour	50 mL
1 tsp	vanilla extract	5 mL
¼ tsp	salt	1 mL

Bake Vanilla Crumb Crust as directed but in 8-inch (2 L) springform pan. Spray sides of springform pan above cooled crust with nonstick cooking spray. Place pan on large sheet of foil; press up foil to sides of pan. Wrap up remaining areas with another piece of foil to make pan waterproof.

Strawberry Topping: If strawberry spread is not seedless, press enough through fine sieve to measure ¼ cup (50 mL); set aside. In saucepan, combine cornstarch with water. Add strawberries and SPLENDA® Granular; bring to boil over medium heat, stirring. Simmer 1 minute. Pour into blender; add spread and purée. Set aside.

Batter: In food processor or blender with sharp blade, process ricotta cheese until smooth. Add cream cheese, SPLENDA® Granular, yogurt, eggs, flour, vanilla and salt; process until smooth. Pour over crust. Drop spoonfuls of strawberry purée carefully over top. Using knife, swirl lightly to create marbled effect.

Place pan in large baking pan. Pour in enough boiling water to come about 1 inch (2.5 cm) up sides. Bake in 325°F (160°C) oven for 1 hour. Reduce heat to 300°F (150°C); bake 10 minutes or until strawberry marble areas are just set.

Turn off oven and prop door open. Run thin knife between cheesecake and pan to allow steam to escape. Return cheesecake to oven, close door and allow cheesecake to cool completely. Cover and refrigerate.

Yield: 12 servings.

---

1 serving:
207 calories, 10.1 g protein, 10.2 g fat, 18.6 g carbohydrate, 0.7 g fiber
½ ■ + ½ ▰ + ½ ◆ Skim + 1 ◉ + 1½ ▲

Can we have our cheesecake and eat it too?

Here's a revealing comparison between a regular Strawberry Marble Cheesecake and the SPLENDA® Granular low-fat version.

	Calories per serving	Fat grams per serving
Regular Cheesecake	523	31
SPLENDA® Granular Cheesecake	207	10
Reductions in calories and fat (per serving)	316	21

1 serving of regular strawberry cheesecake:
523 calories, 8.2 g protein, 31.2 g fat, 54.6 g carbohydrate, 1.9 g fiber

---

Pies and Pastries

Single Pie Crust

A lighter version of my never-fail recipe from my first book, Splendid Desserts. *Spraying the pie plate with nonstick cooking spray will allow easier removal of pie slices and at times the whole cooled pie can be lifted out of the pie dish and placed on an attractive serving plate. For alternative crusts, see page 61 or 66.*

1 cup	all-purpose flour	250 mL
2 tbsp	diet margarine	25 mL
2 tbsp	butter or margarine, softened	25 mL
¼ tsp	baking powder	1 mL
¼ tsp	salt	1 mL
3 tbsp	cold water	45 mL
1 tsp	vinegar	5 mL

In food processor, combine flour, diet margarine, butter, baking powder and salt; process on low speed until mixture resembles crumbs. Combine water and vinegar; add gradually while food processor is on. Turn out onto lightly floured surface. Shape into ball; flatten into disk.

Roll out to 11 to 12-inch (28 to 30 cm) circle. Spray 9-inch (23 cm) glass pie dish lightly with nonstick cooking spray, if desired. Line dish with pastry, trimming to ½ inch (1 cm) border beyond edge. Fold border under and flute.

Prick crust all over with fork to prevent lifting while baking. Bake in 400°F (200°C) oven for approximately 15 minutes or until lightly browned. Cool before filling.

Yield: 1 baked 9-inch (23 cm) pie crust, 8 servings.

Variation:
Chocolate Single Pie Crust: Replace 1 cup (250 mL) all-purpose flour with ¾ cup (175 mL) all-purpose flour, ¼ cup (50 mL) cocoa and ¼ cup (50 mL) SPLENDA® Granular (see Helpful Hints, page 3).

---

1 serving Single Pie Crust:
95 calories, 1.7 g protein, 4.4 g fat, 12.0 g carbohydrate, 0.5 g fiber
1 ■ + 1 ▲

1 serving Chocolate Single Pie Crust:
92 calories, 1.7 g protein, 5.1 g fat, 11.1 g carbohydrate, 1.3 g fiber
½ ■ + 1 ▲ + 1 ♯♯

Apple Crumble Pie

My two boys liked this pie. The pie was happily devoured before their dad even had a chance to sample it.

unbaked Single Pie Crust, page 56

Filling:

6 cups	sliced peeled apples	1.5 L
2 tbsp	lemon juice	25 mL
⅔ cup	SPLENDA® Granular	150 mL
2 tbsp	all-purpose flour	25 mL
½ tsp	cinnamon	2 mL
⅛ tsp	grated nutmeg	0.5 mL

Topping:

⅓ cup	all-purpose flour	75 mL
⅓ cup	rolled oats	75 mL
⅓ cup	SPLENDA® Granular	75 mL
1 tsp	cinnamon	5 mL
3 tbsp	diet margarine	45 mL

Prepare crust as directed, but do not bake.

Filling: In medium bowl, toss apples with lemon juice. In small bowl, combine SPLENDA® Granular, flour, cinnamon and nutmeg; stir into apples. Layer apples neatly on prepared crust.

Topping: In small bowl, combine flour, oats, SPLENDA® Granular and cinnamon. With fork, cut in margarine until mixture is crumbly. Sprinkle over apples. Bake in 425°F (220°C) oven for 15 minutes. Reduce heat to 350°F (180°C); bake for further 30 to 35 minutes or until apples are tender. If pie browns too quickly, cover loosely with foil.

Yield: 8 servings.

---

1 serving:
214 calories, 3.1 g protein, 7.1 g fat, 35.6 g carbohydrate, 3.1 g fiber
1½ ▣ + 1 ◨ + 1½ ▲

Rhubarb Strawberry Crumble Pie

This combination of fruit is a Canadian favorite.

unbaked Single Pie Crust, page 56

Filling:

1	pkg (20 oz/600 g) frozen unsweetened rhubarb/strawberry blend	1
1 cup	SPLENDA® Granular	250 mL
3 tbsp	cornstarch	45 mL
3 tbsp	cold water	45 mL
1 tsp	vanilla extract	5 mL

Topping:

⅓ cup	all-purpose flour	75 mL
⅓ cup	rolled oats	75 mL
⅓ cup	SPLENDA® Granular	75 mL
1 tsp	cinnamon	5 mL
3 tbsp	diet margarine	45 mL

Prepare crust as directed, but do not bake.

Filling: Defrost fruit partially. In medium saucepan, stir SPLENDA® Granular into fruit. In cup, stir cornstarch into cold water to form smooth paste; add to fruit and bring to boil over medium heat, stirring. Stir in vanilla. Allow to cool slightly; pour into prepared crust.

Topping: In small bowl, combine flour, oats, SPLENDA® Granular and cinnamon. With fork cut in margarine until mixture is crumbly. Sprinkle over fruit. Bake in 375°F (190°C) oven for 35 to 40 minutes. Cover loosely with foil as soon as crust is brown enough.

Yield: 8 servings.

---

1 serving:
195 calories, 3.2 g protein, 6.9 g fat, 30.3 g carbohydrate, 2.4 g fiber
1½ ■ + ½ ◢ + 1½ ▲

Pecan Pie

This pie, although different from traditional pecan pie, is delicious.
Serve plain or with low-calorie dessert topping.

unbaked Single Pie Crust, page 56

Syrup:

1¾ cups	SPLENDA® Granular	425 mL
¾ cup	pineapple juice	175 mL
¼ cup	granulated fructose (see page 5)	50 mL
1 tbsp	cornstarch	15 mL
1 tbsp	butter or margarine	15 mL
⅛ tsp	salt	0.5 mL
1 tsp	vanilla extract	5 mL

Filling:

1½ cups	pecan halves	375 mL
2	eggs	2
1 cup	SPLENDA® Granular	250 mL
⅓ cup	butter or margarine, melted	75 mL

Prepare crust as directed, but do not bake.

Syrup: In medium saucepan, stir together SPLENDA® Granular, pineapple juice, fructose, cornstarch, butter and salt; bring to boil over medium heat. Remove from heat. Stir in vanilla. Allow to cool slightly.

Filling: Place pecans in pie crust. In bowl, beat eggs lightly; stir in SPLENDA® Granular, butter and syrup. Pour over pecans. Bake in 375°F (190°C) oven for 15 minutes. Reduce heat to 350°F (180°C); bake for further 30 minutes or until center is softly set.

Yield: 12 servings.

---

1 serving:
272 calories, 3.3 g protein, 19.2 g fat, 23.1 g carbohydrate, 1.2 g fiber
½ ■ + ½ ◨ + 1 ✱ + 4 ▲

Thanksgiving Pumpkin Pie

This is every bit as good as the real thing!

	unbaked Single Pie Crust, page 56	

Filling:

2	eggs	2
1	can (14 oz/398 mL) pumpkin purée	1
1¼ cups	evaporated skim milk	300 mL
1 cup	SPLENDA® Granular	250 mL
1 tsp	cinnamon	5 mL
½ tsp	ground ginger	2 mL
¼ tsp	grated nutmeg	1 mL
⅛ tsp	ground cloves	0.5 mL
⅛ tsp	salt	0.5 mL

Topping:

2 cups	prepared low-calorie dessert topping (see page 5)	500 mL

Prepare crust as directed in deep pie dish, but do not bake.

Filling: In large bowl, beat eggs. Add pumpkin, milk, SPLENDA® Granular, cinnamon, ginger, nutmeg, cloves and salt; beat with wire whisk until combined. Pour over crust. Bake in 450°F (230°C) oven for 10 minutes. Reduce heat to 350°F (180°C); bake for further 30 minutes or until set. Cover loosely with foil as soon as crust is brown enough. Allow to cool. Spread topping over pie.

Yield: 8 servings.

---

1 serving:
200 calories, 7.6 g protein, 7.5 g fat, 26.4 g carbohydrate, 1.5 g fiber
1 ■ + ½ ◩ + ½ ◆ Skim + 1½ ▲

No-Bake Strawberry Cheesecake (p. 43), Harvest Pear Tart (p. 70) and Cream Puff (p. 74)

Double Pie Crust

My mother-in-law, Kay Eloff, gave me this jewel of a recipe. See Apricot-Peach Lattice Pie, on page 62, for instructions on using this recipe for a lattice pie (see Helpful Hints, page 3).

2 cups	all-purpose flour	500 mL
2 tbsp	SPLENDA® Granular	25 mL
1 tsp	baking powder	5 mL
½ tsp	salt	2 mL
1	egg	1
½ cup	skim milk	125 mL
¼ cup	vegetable oil	50 mL

In medium bowl, combine flour, SPLENDA® Granular, baking powder and salt. In small bowl, beat egg; stir in milk and oil. Stir into dry ingredients with fork. Knead lightly; shape into 2 equal balls.

Roll out to fit two 9-inch (23 cm) glass pie dishes. Prick dough all over with fork to prevent lifting while baking. Bake in 350°F (180°C) oven for 20 minutes or until turning golden brown.

Yield: 2 baked single 9-inch (23 cm) pie crusts or 1 double crust.

Note: If desired, freeze extra unbaked pie crust. Use freezer wrap and foil to seal completely. If you will be using this recipe for a single crust, the nutritional analysis will be half of the values indicated.

---

1 serving Double Pie Crust (⅛ of recipe):
191 calories, 4.5 g protein, 7.8 g fat, 25.2 g carbohydrate, 1.0 g fiber
1½ ■ + 1½ ▲ + 1 ++

(top) Honeydew Apple Cream (p. 80)
and Summer Fruit Cobbler (p. 81)
(clockwise from top left) Oh, Choco-
late! (p. 91), Apricot Balls (p. 94)
and Truffles (p. 92)

Apricot-Peach Lattice Pie

This fabulous pie tastes like a fresh fruit pie! When cooled, this pie can be lifted right out of the pie dish and placed on a pretty serving platter.

pastry for Double Pie Crust, page 61

Filling:

2 cups	dried apricots, cut in half	500 mL
2	cans (14 oz/398 mL each) sliced peaches in juice	2
¾ cup	SPLENDA® Granular	175 mL
1 tbsp	lemon juice	15 mL
1 tbsp	cornstarch	15 mL

Prepare pastry as directed; shape into 2 balls, 1 a little larger than the other. Roll out larger ball into 11 to 12 inch (28 to 30 cm) circle; roll out smaller ball into 9 to 10-inch (23 to 25 cm) circle. Line deep 9-inch (23 cm) pie dish with larger circle; trim edge.

Filling: Pour boiling water over apricots to cover. Let stand 1 hour; drain. Drain peaches, reserving juice in medium saucepan. Add apricots, SPLENDA® Granular and lemon juice; bring to boil. Reduce heat, cover and simmer for 20 minutes or until about ⅔ cup (150 mL) liquid remains. In cup, add cornstarch to small amount of liquid; return to saucepan and stir well. Add peaches; allow to cool slightly. Spoon into pie shell.

With fluted pastry cutter or knife, cut ½-inch (1 cm) wide strips out of small pastry circle (or use lattice pastry cutter). Weave strips over filling in lattice pattern. Bake in 375°F (190°C) oven approximately 35 minutes or until crust is golden brown. Serve warm or at room temperature.

Yield: 8 servings.

---

1 serving:
328 calories, 6.4 g protein, 8.0 g fat, 60.6 g carbohydrate, 5.1 g fiber
1½ ▪ + 3½ ◢ + 1½ ▲

Lattice Fruit Pies

Fruit	Quantity of Fruit	SPLENDA® Granular	All-Purpose Flour	Spices or Flavoring
Rhubarb, cut into 1-inch (2.5 cm) pieces	5 cups (1.25 L)	1-1/2 cups (375 mL)	1/4 cup (50 mL)	1 tsp (5 mL) vanilla extract
Apples, peeled, cored and cut into thin slices	8 cups (2 L)	2/3 cup (150 mL)	2 tbsp (25 mL)	1/2 tsp (2 mL) cinnamon 1/8 tsp (0.5 mL) grated nutmeg
Peaches, peeled, pitted and cut into thin slices	6 cups (1.5 L)	3/4 cup (175 mL)	3 tbsp (45 mL)	1 tsp (5 mL) finely grated lemon rind
Nectarines, pitted and cut into thin slices	6 cups (1.5 L)	3/4 cup (175 mL)	3 tbsp (45 mL)	1 tsp (5 mL) finely grated lemon rind
Pears	6 cups (1.5 L)	1/2 cup (125 mL)	1/4 cup (50 mL)	4 tsp (20 mL) lemon juice
Frozen berry mix OR mixed berries (Bumbleberry)	1 pkg (600 g) 5 cups (1.25 L)	3/4 cup (175 mL)	1/4 cup (50 mL)	1 tbsp (15 mL) lemon juice
Raspberries	5 cups (1.25 L)	3/4 cup (175 mL)	1/4 cup (50 mL)	1/4 tsp (1 mL) almond extract
Apricots, pitted and thinly sliced	5 cups (1.25 L)	1-1/2 cups (375 mL)	6 tbsp (90 mL)	1 tsp (5 mL) finely grated lemon rind
Blueberries OR Saskatoons	5 cups (1.25 L)	1 cup (250 mL)	3 tbsp (45 mL)	1 tsp (5 mL) finely grated lemon rind
Strawberries, thinly sliced	6 cups (1.5 L)	1/2 cup (125 mL)	1/4 cup (50 mL)	1 tbsp (15 mL) lemon juice
Sweet cherries, pitted	5 cups (1.25 L)	1-1/4 cups (300 mL)	1/3 cup (75 mL)	1/4 tsp (1 mL) cherry or almond extract
Prune plums, pitted and thinly sliced	4 cups (1 L)	1 cup (250 mL)	3 tbsp (45 mL)	2 tsp (10 mL) lemon juice

If using frozen fruit, partially thaw the fruit. Toss fruit with lemon juice (if using) and with a mixture of SPLENDA® Granular, flour and spices. Place fruit in a pastry-lined 9-inch (23 cm) pie plate. Dot with 1 tbsp (15 mL) diet margarine. Top fruit with a latticework of remaining pastry. Bake in 450°F (230°C) oven for 15 minutes; reduce heat to 350°F (180°C) and bake a further 40 minutes or until fruit is tender. Cover pie with a foil tent, if necessary, to prevent over browning.

Yield: 8 servings.

Note: The nutritional analysis for the Double Pie Crust is on page 61, however, the analysis for the fruit filling per slice of pie will be different for each variation.

Apple Pizza Pie

This innovative pie may be sliced and eaten just like pizza.

pastry for Double Pie Crust, page 61

Filling:

¾ cup	unsweetened applesauce	175 mL
1 tbsp	SPLENDA® Granular	15 mL
6 or 7	medium-size Golden Delicious or Granny Smith apples	6 or 7
¼ cup	lemon juice	50 mL
½ cup	SPLENDA® Granular	125 mL
1 tsp	cinnamon	5 mL

Topping:

¾ cup	all-purpose flour	175 mL
½ cup	SPLENDA® Granular	125 mL
¼ cup	diet margarine, melted	50 mL

Prepare pastry as directed; roll out to fit 12-inch (30 cm) pizza pan and leave 1-inch (2.5 cm) overhang. Fold overhang under; flute with fingers, making nice raised edge.

Filling: In small bowl, combine applesauce with 1 tbsp (15 mL) SPLENDA® Granular; spread over crust. Peel, core and slice apples thinly into medium bowl; toss with lemon juice. Place 1 layer of apples neatly over applesauce. In small bowl, combine ½ cup (125 mL) SPLENDA® Granular with cinnamon; sprinkle half over apples. Layer remaining apples over top; sprinkle with remaining cinnamon mixture.

Topping: In small bowl, stir flour with SPLENDA® Granular; stir in margarine with fork until crumbly. Sprinkle over apples. Bake in 450°F (230°C) oven for 10 minutes. Reduce heat to 350°F (180°C); bake for further 30 minutes or until apples are tender. Cover lightly with foil to prevent overbrowning. Serve warm or at room temperature.

Yield: 12 servings.

---

1 serving:
226 calories, 4.0 g protein, 7.3 g fat, 36.7 g carbohydrate, 2.7 g fiber
1 ■ + 2 ▰ + 1½ ▲

Graham Crumb Crust for Pies

Grape-Nuts cereal has no added sugar or fat. The Grape-Nuts cereal may be replaced with graham cracker crumbs (see Helpful Hints, page 3).

⅔ cup	Grape-Nuts cereal OR graham cracker crumbs	150 mL
⅔ cup	graham cracker crumbs	150 mL
⅓ cup	SPLENDA® Granular	75 mL
¼ cup	diet margarine, melted	50 mL

In blender or small food grinder, blend Grape-Nuts cereal into fine crumbs; transfer to bowl. Stir in graham cracker crumbs and SPLENDA® Granular. Stir in margarine with fork. Press into 9-inch (23 cm) glass pie dish and 1-inch (2.5 cm) up sides. Bake in 350°F (180°C) oven for 10 minutes. Cool.

Yield: 1 nine-inch (23 cm) pie crust, 8 servings.

Variations:

Oreo Crumb Crust for Pies: Substitute ½ cup (125 mL) Oreo crumbs for the graham cracker crumbs. Add 1 tbsp (15 mL) cocoa and 1 extra tbsp (15 mL) SPLENDA® Granular.

Vanilla Crumb Crust for Pies: Substitute crushed vanilla wafers for the graham cracker crumbs.

---

1 serving Graham Crumb Crust:
98 calories, 1.9 g protein, 3.7 g fat, 15.3 g carbohydrate, 1.3 g fiber
1 ▣ + 1 ▲

1 serving Oreo Crumb Crust:
95 calories, 1.8 g protein, 4.1 g fat, 13.5 g carbohydrate, 1.4 g fiber
½ ▣ + ½ ✳ + 1 ▲

1 serving Vanilla Crumb Crust:
97 calories, 1.6 g protein, 4.0 g fat, 14.0 g carbohydrate, 1.1 g fiber
1 ▣ + 1 ▲

Crunchy Almond Crust

This flavorful crust can be used in place of graham crusts as well as the single pie crust to add interest to just about any open pie or fruit tart. (See Helpful Hints, page 3.)

½ cup	slivered almonds	125 mL
¾ cup	all-purpose flour	175 mL
⅓ cup	SPLENDA® Granular	75 mL
2 tbsp	diet margarine	25 mL
2	egg whites	2
¼ tsp	almond extract	1 mL

In nonstick skillet, toast almonds over medium heat, stirring to prevent burning. In food processor, combine almonds, flour, SPLENDA® Granular and margarine; process until almonds are coarsely chopped. Add egg whites and almond extract; process until ball forms. Press into 9-inch (23 cm) pie plate; prick all over with fork. Bake in 375°F (190°C) oven for 15 minutes.

Yield: 1 nine-inch (23 cm) pie crust.

---

1 serving:
119 calories, 4.0 g protein, 6.5 g fat, 11.9 g carbohydrate, 1.0 g fiber
½ ■ + ½ ✳ + ½ ◯ + 1 ▲

Key Lime Pie

Our dear friends, Dick and Mary, really enjoyed this pie when they spent
Christmas with us in 1994. Make one day ahead.

Graham Crumb Crust for Pies, page 65

Filling:

⅔ cup	SPLENDA® Granular Condensed Milk, page 114	150 mL
½ cup	skim milk powder	125 mL
½ cup	SPLENDA® Granular	125 mL
½ cup	lime juice	125 mL
⅓ cup	water	75 mL
3	egg yolks	3
1	drop green food coloring	1

Topping:

2 cups	prepared low-calorie dessert topping (see page 5)	500 mL
	Lime slice	

Prepare crust as directed.

Filling: In food processor or blender, combine SPLENDA® Granular Condensed Milk, skim milk powder, SPLENDA® Granular, lime juice, water, egg yolks and green food coloring; process until smooth. Pour over baked crust. Bake in 325°F (160°C) oven for approximately 30 minutes or until set. Let cool.

Topping: Spread dessert topping over cooled pie. Garnish with twisted lime slice. Chill.

Yield: 8 servings.

---

1 serving:
236 calories, 8.3 g protein, 10.0 g fat, 29.8 g carbohydrate, 1.3 g fat
1 ■ + 1½ ◆ Skim + ½ ✱ + 2 ▲

Lemon Meringue Pie

Refreshing lemon flavor.

Single Pie Crust, page 56

Filling:

1 cup	SPLENDA® Granular	250 mL
¼ cup	cornstarch	50 mL
⅛ tsp	salt	0.5 mL
2	egg yolks	2
2 cups	hot water	500 mL
⅓ cup	lemon juice	75 mL
1 tbsp	diet margarine	15 mL
dash	yellow food coloring (optional)	dash

Meringue:

⅓ cup	all-fruit apricot spread (see page 5)	75 mL
3 tbsp	water	45 mL
1 tbsp	SPLENDA® Granular	15 mL
1 tbsp	cornstarch	15 mL
4	egg whites, at room temperature	4
¼ tsp	cream of tartar	1 mL

Prepare crust as directed.

Filling: In saucepan, combine SPLENDA® Granular, cornstarch and salt; stir in egg yolks. Gradually stir in hot water; cook over medium heat, stirring, until boiling and thickened. Remove from heat. Stir in lemon juice, margarine and food coloring, if using. Cool slightly; pour over baked crust.

Meringue: In blender, blend apricot spread and water until smooth. In small saucepan, combine apricot mixture, SPLENDA® Granular and cornstarch; bring to boil. Set aside in refrigerator to cool. In bowl, beat egg whites until frothy; add cream of tartar and beat 1 minute. Add apricot mixture; beat until stiff peaks form. Spread over filling, sealing well to pastry rim. Bake in 350°F (180°C) oven for 10 to 15 minutes or until nicely browned in places.

Yield: 8 servings.

---

1 serving:
168 calories, 4.3 g protein, 6.5 g fat, 22.8 g carbohydrate, 0.6 g fiber
1 ▣ + ½ ✳ + 1½ ▲

Frozen Grasshopper Pie

This dessert has been tested on many friends and everyone agrees it is delicious! Garnish with Chocolate Curls, below, if desired.

	Oreo Crumb Crust, page 65	
Filling:		
⅔ cup	SPLENDA® Granular Condensed Milk, page 114	150 mL
1 tsp	peppermint extract	5 mL
8	drops green food coloring	8
4 cups	prepared low-calorie dessert topping (see page 5)	1 L

Prepare crust as directed.

Filling: In blender, combine SPLENDA® Granular Condensed Milk, peppermint extract and food coloring until blended. Pour into bowl; fold in dessert topping. Pour into cooled crust. Freeze for 6 hours or until firm. Cover with plastic wrap and foil; freeze no longer than 5 days.

Yield: 8 servings.

---

1 serving:
212 calories, 6.3 g protein, 9.9 g fat, 25.5 g carbohydrate, 1.4 g fiber
½ ▣ + 1 ◆ Skim + 1 ✳ + 2 ▲

Chocolate Curls (optional): Microwave 1 oz (30 g) bittersweet chocolate just until soft. Spread the chocolate thinly with a knife over a small flat baking sheet or dinner plate. Freeze until firm enough to form curls when knife is dragged firmly across surface. If chocolate freezes too hard, curls will not form. Leave pan at room temperature for a few minutes and try again.

Harvest Pear Tart

A great way to use those ripe pears before they spoil. (Pictured opposite page 60.)

Single Pie Crust, page 56

Filling:

8	medium-size ripe pears	8
½ cup	SPLENDA® Granular	125 mL
¼ tsp	ground ginger	1 mL
¼ tsp	cinnamon	1 mL
2	cans (14 oz/398 mL each) sliced pears in pear juice, drained	2

Glaze:

3 tbsp	all-fruit apricot spread (see page 5)	45 mL
1½ tsp	water	7 mL

Prepare crust as directed. Use any leftover pastry to cut out several small leaf shapes for garnish. Bake the crust in a 400°F (200°C) oven for 15 minutes and bake the leaves separately on a small baking sheet for 8 minutes.

Filling: Peel and slice fresh pears; process in food processor or blender with metal blade until almost smooth. Transfer to medium saucepan with heavy bottom; stir in SPLENDA® Granular, ginger and cinnamon. Bring to boil over medium heat; reduce heat to medium-low and cook until very thick and all liquid has evaporated. Allow to cool. Pour into baked crust. Arrange pear slices on top.

Glaze: In small saucepan, heat apricot spread with water until melted. Press through sieve. Brush over pear slices. Garnish the tart with the pastry leaves. Refrigerate.

Yield: 8 servings.

---

1 serving:
221 calories, 2.5 g protein, 5.1 g fat, 44.0 g carbohydrate, 4.6 g fiber
1 ■ + 2½ ● + 1 ▲

Pear Strudel

A wonderful variation of the popular apple strudel dessert. Serve warm with dessert topping or ice cream, if desired.

4	large fresh pears, peeled and sliced	4
1 tsp	lemon juice	5 mL
½ cup	SPLENDA® Granular	125 mL
1 tsp	cornstarch	5 mL
¼ tsp	ground ginger	1 mL
⅛ tsp	cinnamon	0.5 mL
2	slices white bread, toasted	2
¼ cup	finely chopped almonds OR walnuts	50 mL
6	sheets phyllo pastry	6
2 tbsp	SPLENDA® Granular	25 mL

In bowl, toss pears with lemon juice. In small bowl, combine SPLENDA® Granular, cornstarch, ginger and cinnamon; sprinkle over pears. Crumble toast in blender to make crumbs; stir into pear mixture. Stir in nuts.

Keeping remaining phyllo covered with damp towel to prevent drying out, place 1 sheet on large piece of waxed paper. Spray with buttery flavor nonstick cooking spray; sprinkle with 1 tsp (5 mL) SPLENDA® Granular. Repeat layering with remaining phyllo and SPLENDA® Granular.

Place filling in center of phyllo. Using waxed paper, roll up jelly-roll style. Carefully place, seam side down, on greased cookie sheet. Tuck in ends. Cut a few evenly spaced slits on surface. Bake in 350°F (180°C) oven for 30 to 35 minutes or until golden brown. If pastry browns too quickly, cover loosely with foil.

Yield: 8 servings.

---

1 serving:
157 calories, 3.5 g protein, 3.1 g fat, 30.5 g carbohydrate, 2.5 g fiber
1 ▇ + 1½ ▰ + ½ ▲

Cranapple Pie in Phyllo

An unusual, gorgeous festive pie, actually quite easy and fun to make. Golden Delicious apples work well in this recipe. This dessert is lovely served warm with dessert topping.

8 cups	sliced peeled apples	2 L
1¼ cups	frozen cranberries	300 mL
¾ cup	SPLENDA® Granular	175 mL
¼ cup	all-purpose flour	50 mL
1 tsp	cinnamon	5 mL
⅛ tsp	grated nutmeg	0.5 mL
2	slices white bread, toasted	2
⅓ cup	finely chopped walnuts	75 mL
8	sheets phyllo pastry	8
½ cup	diet margarine, melted	125 mL

In bowl, combine apples, cranberries, SPLENDA® Granular, flour, cinnamon and nutmeg; set aside. Crumble toast in blender to make crumbs; stir in walnuts.

Keeping remaining phyllo covered with damp towel to prevent drying out, place 1 sheet on work surface. Brush with some of the margarine; sprinkle 2 heaping teaspoons (10 mL) of the bread mixture over one half crosswise. Fold uncovered half over crumb mixture. Brush both sides with margarine. Place 1 short end of phyllo in center of 9-inch (2.5 L) springform pan, leaving other end dangling over edge. Sprinkle 1½ tsp (7 mL) crumbs over phyllo in pan.

Repeat with remaining phyllo sheets, overlapping carefully in pan to completely cover pan. Sprinkle with remaining crumbs. Place apple mixture over top. Carefully fold each phyllo sheet over filling to cover.

Bake on lowest rack of 375°F (190°C) oven for 10 minutes. Cover with foil as soon as slightly browned. Reduce heat to 350°F (180°C); bake a further 55 minutes. Allow to cool in pan on rack. Remove sides of pan.

Yield: 12 servings.

---

1 serving:
177 calories, 2.9 g protein, 6.7 g fat, 28.0 g carbohydrate, 2.7 g fiber
1 ⬛ + 1 ◢ + 1½ ▲

Apple Danish

These are a favorite of my oldest son, Daniel. Golden Delicious or McIntosh apples work well in this recipe.

1 cup	butter-flavored shortening	250 mL
3 cups	all-purpose flour	750 mL
1 tsp	salt	5 mL
⅔ cup	skim milk	150 mL
1	egg yolk	1

Filling:

1 cup	SPLENDA® Granular	250 mL
1 tbsp	all-purpose flour	15 mL
1 tsp	cinnamon	5 mL
7½ cups	sliced peeled apples	1.9 L
2 tbsp	diet margarine	25 mL

Glaze:

1	egg white	1

In food processor fitted with dough blade, process shortening until softened. Add flour and salt; process until combined. Stir milk with egg yolk; add to flour mixture and process until dough begins to cling together. Knead lightly. Divide in half. On lightly floured surface, roll out each half to 15 x 10-inch (38 x 25 cm) rectangle; line same size jelly-roll pan with 1 of the rectangles.

Filling: In small bowl, combine SPLENDA® Granular, flour and cinnamon; sprinkle over apples in separate bowl and stir to mix well. Arrange apples over pastry; dot with margarine. Cover with remaining pastry.

Glaze: Beat egg white until frothy; brush over pastry. Bake in 350°F (180°C) oven for 40 minutes or until golden brown. Serve warm or at room temperature.

Yield: 24 bars.

---

1 bar:
165 calories, 2.2 g protein, 9.2 g fat, 18.7 g carbohydrate, 1.3 g fiber
1 ▣ + 2 ▲ +1 ⊞

Cream Puffs

These are easy and fun to make. The fat is reduced by replacing some of the butter with diet margarine. (Pictured opposite page 60.)

1 cup	water	250 mL
⅓ cup	diet margarine	75 mL
3 tbsp	butter or margarine	45 mL
1½ cups	all-purpose flour	375 mL
⅛ tsp	salt	0.5 mL
4	large eggs	4
2 cups	Strawberry Whipped Topping, page 111	500 mL

Spray a cookie sheet with nonstick cooking spray; set aside. In medium saucepan, combine 1 cup (250 mL) water, margarine and butter; bring to boil. Remove from heat. Stir in flour and salt all at once. Stir in eggs, 1 at a time, beating with wooden spoon after each addition until smooth.

Spoon into pastry bag with ½-inch (1 cm) front opening; secure bag with ring. (Do not worry about tip unless you have plain tip of this size.) Pipe sixteen 2-inch (5 cm) rounds onto prepared cookie sheet.

Bake in 450°F (230°C) oven for 15 minutes. Reduce heat to 350°F (180°C); bake a further 10 to 15 minutes or until puffed and golden brown. Cool completely on wire rack. Split in half and remove any soft dough from inside. Fill each with about 2 tbsp (25 mL) Strawberry Whipped Topping.

Yield: 16 Cream Puffs.

Variation:
Eclairs: For each eclair, pipe 2 strips 4 inches (10 cm) long and ½ inch (1 cm) wide side by side, on cookie sheet. Pipe another 2 strips on top, making eclair almost 1 inch (2.5 cm) high. Bake and fill as directed. Glaze with 1 tbsp (15 mL) Chocolate Fudge Topping, page 111.

Yield: 9 Eclairs.

---

1 cream puff:
108 calories, 3.1 g protein, 5.9 g fat, 10.5 g carbohydrate, 0.4 g fiber
½ ■ + ½ ● + 1 ▲ + 1 ╉

1 eclair:
209 calories, 6.1 g protein, 11.2 g fat, 21.5 g carbohydrate, 1.6 g fiber
1 ■ + ½ ✱ + ½ ● + 2 ▲

Puddings, Trifles and Frozen Desserts

Steamed Chocolate Pudding

This cake pudding rises high and is a lovely dessert served with hot Rum Custard Sauce, page 115.

½ cup	raisins	125 mL
1 tsp	rum extract	5 mL
⅓ cup	butter or margarine, softened	75 mL
1	egg	1
1 cup	SPLENDA® Granular	250 mL
2 cups	all-purpose flour	500 mL
½ cup	cocoa	125 mL
5 tsp	baking powder	25 mL
1¼ cups	skim milk	300 mL
2 cups	Rum Custard Sauce, page 115	500 mL

With scissors, snip raisins in half; place in small microwaveable dish. Cover with water and lid; microwave 2 minutes at High. Drain and stir in rum extract. Set aside.

In bowl, beat together butter, egg and SPLENDA® Granular. In separate bowl, sift together flour, cocoa and baking powder; add to butter mixture alternately with milk, beating on low speed until combined. Stir in raisins.

Spoon into greased 8-cup (2 L) mold; cover with lid, preferably domed. Place on rack in deep kettle. Pour in enough boiling water to come 1 inch (2.5 cm) up side of mold. Place lid on kettle; steam over medium-low heat for approximately 2 hours or until cake tester inserted in center comes out clean. Top up the boiling water when necessary.

Allow to cool 10 minutes. Run knife between pudding and mold; invert and gently remove. Serve immediately with Rum Custard Sauce.

Yield: 12 servings.

Note: Any leftover pudding can be wrapped in plastic wrap and foil and refrigerated.

To reheat, remove plastic wrap and cover pudding completely in foil. Bake in 350°F (180°C) oven for 35 to 45 minutes (for entire pudding), or until heated through for leftover pudding.

1 serving:

208 calories, 5.9 g protein, 7.3 g fat, 31.4 g carbohydrate, 2.2 g fiber

1 ■ + ½ ◩ + ½ ◆ Skim + ½ ✱ + 1½ ▲

Coffee Banana-Nut Pudding

This lovely coffee-flavored pudding is a great time saver.

1 tsp	instant coffee granules	5 mL
2 tsp	hot water	10 mL
1½ cups	skim milk	375 mL
½ cup	half-and-half cream	125 mL
½ cup	SPLENDA® Granular	125 mL
1	pkg (30 g) instant light vanilla pudding (see page 5)	1
1 cup	prepared low-calorie dessert topping (see page 5)	250 mL
2	medium bananas, sliced	2
2 tbsp	lemon juice	25 mL
3 tbsp	finely chopped nuts	45 mL

In large bowl, dissolve coffee in hot water; stir in milk, cream and SPLENDA® Granular. Add instant pudding; beat on low speed until thickened. Fold in dessert topping.

Sprinkle sliced bananas with lemon juice; pat dry with paper towel. Stir into pudding along with 2 tbsp (25 mL) of the nuts. Pour into 4 individual pudding bowls. Sprinkle with remaining nuts. Serve immediately or chill for up to 2 hours.

Yield: 4 servings.

---

1 serving:
217 calories, 6.3 g protein, 8.2 g fat, 32.0 g carbohydrate, 1.2 g fiber
1½ 🟦 + 1 ◆ Skim + 1 ✳ + 1½ ▲

77

Bread and Butter Pudding

I modified the recipe my mother-in-law, Kay Eloff, uses to make it lower in fat. Whole wheat bread may be used, if preferred. Serve with Rum Custard Sauce, page 115, if desired.

8	slices (½ inch/1 cm thick) white bread	8
7 tsp	diet margarine OR butter	35 mL
½ cup	all-fruit apricot spread (see page 5)	125 mL
⅓ cup	seedless raisins	75 mL
⅓ cup	chopped dried apricots	75 mL
4	egg whites	4
1	egg	1
2½ cups	skim milk	625 mL
¼ cup	SPLENDA® Granular	50 mL
1 tsp	vanilla extract	5 mL
⅛ tsp	salt	0.5 mL

Spread bread with margarine, then apricot spread. Cut into fingers. Pack in layers in greased 8-inch (2 L) square glass baking dish, sprinkling layers with raisins and apricots.

In bowl, beat together egg whites, egg, skim milk, SPLENDA® Granular, vanilla and salt; pour over bread. Cover and allow to stand 8 hours or overnight.

Bake, covered, in 300°F (150°C) oven for 45 minutes. Increase heat to 350°F (180°C); uncover and bake a further 20 minutes or until golden brown and puffed up. Serve warm.

Yield: 8 servings.

---

1 serving:

155 calories, 7.1 g protein, 3.0 g fat, 25.0 g carbohydrate, 1.0 g fiber

1 ■ + 1 ◢ + ½ ◐ + ½ ▲

Raspberry Banana Trifle

A colorful version of a popular dessert. This dessert is best prepared early in the day or no more than one day ahead.

1¼ cups	all-purpose flour	300 mL
1½ tsp	baking powder	7 mL
2	eggs	2
1 cup	SPLENDA® Granular	250 mL
1½ tsp	vanilla extract	7 mL
½ cup	skim milk	125 mL
1 tbsp	butter or margarine	15 mL
⅓ cup	all-fruit raspberry spread (see page 5)	75 mL
¼ cup	orange juice	50 mL

Custard:

¼ cup	SPLENDA® Granular	50 mL
3 tbsp	custard powder	45 mL
2 cups	skim milk	500 mL
1½ tsp	vanilla extract	7 mL
2	large ripe bananas, sliced	2
2 tbsp	lemon juice	25 mL

Topping:

2 cups	prepared low-calorie dessert topping	500 mL
⅔ cup	fresh raspberries	150 mL

In small bowl, combine flour and baking powder; set aside. In large bowl, beat eggs well with electric mixer on high speed. Add SPLENDA® Granular and vanilla; beat until combined. In small saucepan, heat milk and butter until butter is melted. Add to egg mixture along with flour mixture in 2 additions, beating each time just until smooth. Scoop into greased 8-inch (2 L) square cake pan. Bake in 350°F (180°C) oven for 20 to 25 minutes or until cake tester inserted in center comes out clean. Let cool on wire rack.

Custard: In saucepan, combine SPLENDA® Granular with custard powder. Gradually stir in milk and bring to boil over medium heat, stirring constantly. Stir in vanilla.

Assembly: Cut cooled cake horizontally in half with serrated knife. Combine raspberry spread and 2 tbsp (25 mL) of the orange juice; spread over 1 layer. Top with other layer, making sandwich; cut into 1-inch (2.5 cm) squares.

Cover bottom of 8-cup (2 L) trifle bowl with half of the squares. Sprinkle with 1 tbsp (15 mL) orange juice. Layer with half the banana slices dipped in lemon juice. Pour half the custard overall. Repeat layers once. Cover with plastic wrap and refrigerate until cool. Garnish with dessert topping and raspberries.

Yield: 10 servings.

---

1 serving:

188 calories, 6.0 g protein, 3.8 g fat, 32.4 g carbohydrate, 1.4 g fiber

1 ⬛ + 1 ◢ + ½ ✳ + ½ ⬤ + ½ ▲

Honeydew Apple Cream

This dessert is a pretty pastel green. It looks lovely garnished with pastel pink Strawberry Whipped Topping, page 111. Add sliced kiwifruit to really throw everyone off the trail! (Pictured opposite page 61.)

2 cups	chopped honeydew melon	500 mL
1	can (14 oz/398 mL) unsweetened applesauce	1
2	envelopes unflavored gelatin	2
¾ cup	SPLENDA® Granular	175 mL
1 cup	skim milk yogurt	250 mL
2	drops green food coloring (optional)	2

In blender, blend honeydew melon with applesauce. In small bowl, soften gelatin in 3 tbsp (45 mL) of the puréed fruit. In saucepan, bring remaining purée to boil over medium heat; add gelatin mixture and SPLENDA® Granular and cook until gelatin is completely dissolved. Pour into medium bowl; refrigerate until just cool to the fingertip.

Beat yogurt, and green food coloring, if desired, into fruit mixture. Spoon into large pudding bowl or 6 small dessert bowls. Refrigerate to chill at least 3 hours.

Yield: 6 servings.

---

1 serving:

90 calories, 4.4 g protein, 0.1 g fat, 18.9 g carbohydrate, 1.5 g fiber

1½ ◢ + ½ ◆ Skim

Summer Fruit Cobbler

My son Jonathan, the Cobbler Gobbler, says this is his favorite dessert. This dessert is extra special served warm with a dollop of whipped topping or a generous serving of Vanilla Ice Cream, page 85. (Pictured opposite page 61.)

1	pkg (20 oz/600 g) frozen unsweetened peaches, strawberries and blueberries	1
⅔ cup	SPLENDA® Granular	150 mL
2 tbsp	cornstarch	25 mL
2 tbsp	lemon juice	25 mL
Topping:		
1½ cups	all-purpose flour	375 mL
½ cup	SPLENDA® Granular	125 mL
2 tsp	baking powder	10 mL
¼ tsp	salt	1 mL
3 tbsp	butter or margarine	45 mL
1	egg	1
½ cup	skim milk	125 mL

In saucepan, combine fruit, SPLENDA® Granular, cornstarch and lemon juice; cook over medium heat, stirring frequently, until boiling and thickened. Pour into 8-inch (2 L) square baking dish.

Topping: In medium bowl, stir together flour, SPLENDA® Granular, baking powder and salt; rub in butter. In small bowl, beat egg lightly with fork; stir in milk. Stir egg mixture into dry ingredients with fork until well combined. Drop in 5 or 6 large spoonfuls onto warm filling. Bake in 375°F (190°C) oven for 25 minutes or until browning slightly.

Yield: 8 servings.

Variations: Use frozen unsweetened strawberries, peaches, blueberries or a rhubarb/strawberry blend. Since the rhubarb/strawberry blend is quite tart, replace lemon juice with water and increase SPLENDA® Granular to ¾ cup (175 mL).

---

1 serving:
194 calories, 4.2 g protein, 5.4 g fat, 32.7 g carbohydrate, 2.3 g fiber
1½ ▇ + 1 ◗ + 1 ▲

Tropical Fruit Parfait

Light and refreshing for a lazy summer afternoon treat.

1 tsp	unflavored gelatin	5 mL
1 tsp	cold water	5 mL
1 tbsp	boiling water	15 mL
1	very ripe mango	1
1	ripe banana	1
1 cup	skim milk yogurt	250 mL
½ cup	SPLENDA® Granular	125 mL
½ tsp	coconut extract	2 mL

In small bowl, soak gelatin in 1 tsp (5 mL) cold water. Dissolve in 1 tbsp (15 mL) boiling water. Set aside.

Peel and chop mango and banana. Place in blender along with yogurt, SPLENDA® Granular, coconut extract and gelatin; blend until smooth.

In five 1-cup (250 mL) parfait glasses, layer sliced fruit such as bananas, seedless grapes, kiwifruit, pineapple, mango, papaya, with ½ cup (125 mL) of tropical fruit mixture. Chill.

Yield: 2½ cups (625 mL), or 5 servings.

---

1 serving without layered fruit:
86 calories, 3.5 g protein, 0.3 g fat, 18.5 g carbohydrate, 1.2 g fiber
1½ 🟦 + ½ ◆ Skim

Instant Strawberry Frozen Yogurt

No ice cream maker is required, yet the results are very similar, if not better.

1	pkg (20 oz/600 g) frozen unsweetened strawberries	1
¾ cup	SPLENDA® Granular	175 mL
2 cups	skim milk yogurt	500 mL

If strawberries have any ice crystals, rinse in colander under cold running water briefly; shake off excess. Using food processor with metal blade, process strawberries on lowest speed until chopped and resembling coarsely shaved ice.

Continue processing on medium speed and add SPLENDA® Granular through feed tube. Gradually add yogurt until correct consistency is achieved. Serve immediately. Freeze leftovers in sealed plastic container.

Yield: 10 servings, ½ cup (125 mL) per serving.

---

1 serving:
52 calories, 2.7 g protein, 0.1 g fat, 10.5 g carbohydrate, 0.9 g fiber
½ 🍎 + ½ ◆ Skim

Strawberry-Orange Sherbet

No ice cream maker is required and this virtually fat-free sherbet is always at the correct consistency to serve straight out of the freezer. This is my favorite sherbet.

3 cups	frozen unsweetened strawberries	750 mL
1 cup	orange juice	250 mL
½	can (12 oz/341 mL) frozen orange juice concentrate	½
⅔ cup	SPLENDA® Granular	150 mL
2 tbsp	lemon juice	25 mL

In blender, process strawberries, orange juice, orange juice concentrate, SPLENDA® Granular and lemon juice until smooth. Pour into plastic container with lid; freeze several hours or until frozen.

Yield: 3¾ cups (925 mL), 5 servings, ¾ cup (175 mL) per serving.

Variations:

Strawberry-Pineapple Sherbet: Substitute frozen unsweetened pineapple juice concentrate for the orange juice concentrate and pineapple juice for the orange juice.

Peachy Orange Sherbet: Substitute frozen unsweetened peaches for the strawberries.

Fruit Punch: Place 1 cup (250 mL) Strawberry-Orange Sherbet and 1 cup (250 mL) chilled carbonated water in blender and blend until combined. Serve immediately. Serves 1.

---

1 serving Strawberry-Orange Sherbet:
133 calories, 1.7 g protein, 0.2 g fat, 32.7 g carbohydrate, 1.9 g fiber
3 [🍃]

Vanilla Ice Cream

If a creamier result is desired, use the alternatives suggested. My husband, Ian, prefers the rich version of the chocolate ice cream. He thinks it is the nicest ice cream he has ever tasted! An inexpensive 8-cup (2 L) ice cream maker gives the best results. The Canadian Diabetes Association Food Choice Values and/or Symbols will be different for the variations.

1	can (385 mL) skim evaporated milk, chilled, OR 2% evaporated milk	1
2 tsp	vinegar	10 mL
1½ cups	half-and-half cream	375 mL
2	SPLENDA® Granular Condensed Milk Recipes, page 114 (But use only ¼ cup (50 mL) diet margarine)	2
1 cup	skim milk OR whipping cream	250 mL
1 tbsp	vanilla extract	15 mL

In large bowl, whisk evaporated milk with vinegar until frothy; whisk in cream. Add SPLENDA® Granular Condensed Milk Recipes, skim milk and vanilla. Pour into ice cream maker and freeze according to manufacturer's instructions.

OR freeze in large plastic container, allowing ½ inch (1 cm) for expansion. Freeze a few hours, until mushy. Beat 5 minutes on medium speed. Stir in desired fruit at this stage. Freeze again, stirring occasionally.

Yield: 15 servings, ½ cup (125 mL) per serving.

Variations:
Cappuccino Ice Cream: Dissolve 2 tbsp (25 mL) instant coffee granules in 2 tbsp (25 mL) hot water.
Yield: 15 servings.

Banana Ice Cream: Add 3 cups (750 mL) mashed banana.
Yield: 21 servings.

Strawberry Ice Cream: Add 3 cups (750 mL) strawberries (puréed with some of the milk in a blender).
Yield: 20 servings.

Chocolate Ice Cream: Stir in Chocolate Fudge Topping, page 111. Reduce SPLENDA® Granular to 1½ cups (375 mL) in condensed milk mixture. Stir in 1 oz (30 g) unsweetened chocolate, coarsely grated.
Yield: 18 servings.

Butterscotch Pecan Ice Cream: Add ⅔ cup (150 mL) chopped pecans. Prepare 1 pkg (30 g) light butterscotch pudding (see page 5) as directed and stir in.
Yield: 19 servings.

Mint Chip Ice Cream: Stir in 1 tbsp (15 mL) peppermint extract, 10 drops green food coloring and 1 oz (30 g) unsweetened chocolate, coarsely grated.
Yield: 16 servings.

Maple Walnut Ice Cream: Stir in 1 tsp (5 mL) vanilla, 2 tbsp (25 mL) maple extract and ½ cup (125 mL) chopped walnuts.
Yield: 16 servings.

Hawaiian Ice Cream: Use only 1 recipe for SPLENDA® Granular Condensed Milk. Add 1 can (13.5 oz/400 mL) coconut milk, 1 can (14 oz/398 mL) crushed unsweetened pineapple (drained) and 1 tbsp (15 mL) coconut extract.
Yield: 24 servings.

Peachy Orange Ice Cream: Add 2 cans (each 14 oz/398 mL) unsweetened peaches in juice, drained and blended and ⅔ cup (150 mL) frozen orange juice concentrate.
Yield: 24 servings.

Rum 'n' Raisin Chocolate Pudding Ice Cream: Place ½ cup (125 mL) chopped raisins (cut raisins with scissors) in small bowl; cover with water and lid. Microwave at High for 2 minutes. Drain. Stir in 1 tbsp (15 mL) rum extract. Prepare 1 pkg (40 g) light chocolate pudding (see page 5) as directed and stir in with wire whisk. Add raisins. (Do not omit vanilla extract.)
Yield: 19 servings.

Apricot Ice Cream: Add 3 cups (750 mL) peeled, chopped, apricots, puréed (purée with the skim milk).
Yield: 20 servings.

---

1 serving Vanilla Ice Cream:
135 calories, 7.4 g protein, 4.8 g fat, 15.3 g carbohydrate, 0 g fiber
1 ◆ Skim + 1 ✳ + ½ ◉ + 1 ▲

Chocolate Banana Softserve

This tastes amazingly similar to real ice cream.

5	medium bananas, sliced	5
1 oz	unsweetened chocolate	30 g
½ cup	SPLENDA® Granular Condensed Milk, page 114	125 mL

Freeze bananas overnight.

In small saucepan, melt chocolate over medium heat; stir in SPLENDA® Granular Condensed Milk until smooth. Remove from heat.

If bananas have any ice crystals, rinse in colander under cold running water; shake off excess. In food processor with sharp blade, process frozen bananas on lowest speed, stirring occasionally to push fruit down. Increase speed as soon as possible and continue processing. Add warm chocolate mixture; beat until smooth. Serve immediately or freeze until slightly firmer. If desired, serve in cone cups.

Yield: 4 cups (1 L), ⅓ cup (75 mL) per serving.

Variation:

Chocolate Chunk Banana Softserve: In small saucepan, melt 1 oz (30 g) bittersweet chocolate with the 1 oz (30 g) unsweetened chocolate in recipe; stir and drizzle over bananas. Chop chocolate into little pieces as it begins to harden. Process. To condensed milk mixture, add 2 tbsp (25 mL) cocoa instead of the 1 oz (30 g) unsweetened melted chocolate in recipe.

---

1 serving Chocolate Banana Softserve:
89 calories, 2.3 g protein, 2.9 g fat, 15.6 g carbohydrate, 1.2 g fiber
1 ◼ + ½ ✳ + ½ ▲

1 serving Chocolate Chunk Banana Softserve:
104 calories, 2.6 g protein, 4.1 g fat, 17.2 g carbohydrate, 1.7 g fiber
1 ◼ + ½ ✳ + 1 ▲

Orange Banana Softserve

Incredible flavor, similar to sherbet. Thanks go to my husband, Ian, for suggesting the use of frozen orange juice concentrate!

2½ cups	sliced bananas	625 mL
1 cup	SPLENDA® Granular	250 mL
½	can (12 oz/341 mL) frozen orange juice concentrate	½
1¼ cups	cold plain yogurt	300 mL

Freeze bananas overnight. Using food processor with metal blade, process bananas until coarsely chopped. Add SPLENDA® Granular and orange juice concentrate. While processing, gradually add yogurt through feed tube until correct consistency is achieved. Freeze any leftovers. (Frozen leftovers will be more like regular hard ice cream.)

Yield: 4 cups (1 L), ½ cup (125 mL) per serving.

Variation: Use any other frozen concentrated unsweetened fruit juice of your choice.

---

1 serving:
116 calories, 2.8 g protein, 1.3 g fat, 24.6 g carbohydrate, 1.0 g fiber
2 ◢ + ½ ◆ 2%

Peachy Orange Banana Popsicle

This is Ian's favorite Popsicle treat on a hot summer's day.

1	envelope unflavored gelatin	1
¼ cup	cold water	50 mL
1	can (14 oz/398 mL) unsweetened sliced peaches in juice	1
¾ cup	cold orange juice concentrate, defrosted	175 mL
1 cup	SPLENDA® Granular	250 mL
1	banana, sliced	1

In small saucepan, stir gelatin into ¼ cup (50 mL) cold water; heat over medium heat until dissolved. Pour into blender. Add peaches, orange juice concentrate, SPLENDA® Granular and banana; blend until smooth. Fill Popsicle molds. Freeze.
Yield: 14 Popsicles.

---

1 popsicle:
53 calories, 1.1 g protein, 0.1 g fat, 12.9 g carbohydrate, 0.6 g fiber
1 🍎 + 1 ➕➕

Creamy Fudgsicles

A great little treat with just a hint of banana.

4 cups	prepared low-calorie dessert topping	1 L
1	pkg (40 g) instant light chocolate pudding mix	1
1 cup	skim milk	250 mL
½ cup	mashed banana	125 mL
⅓ cup	SPLENDA® Granular	75 mL
3 tbsp	cocoa	45 mL

In bowl, combine dessert topping, pudding mix, milk, banana, SPLENDA® Granular and cocoa; beat until smooth. Fill Popsicle molds. Freeze.
Yield: 11 fudgsicles.

---

1 fudgsicle:
71 calories, 2.4 g protein, 2.7 g fat, 10.8 g carbohydrate, 0.7 g fiber
½ 🍎 + ½ ✳ + 1 🔺

Confections, Cookies, Brownies and Squares

Oh, Chocolate!

My husband adores this chocolate so much that he asked that I share this unusual recipe. The consistency is that of real chocolate. It is also lower in fat than regular chocolate. (Pictured opposite page 61.)

4 oz	light cream cheese, softened (see page 5)	125 g
5 oz	unsweetened chocolate	150 g
1 tbsp	butter	15 mL
1	pkg (40 g) instant light chocolate pudding, prepared (see page 5)	1
1½ cups	SPLENDA® Granular	375 mL
3 tbsp	granulated fructose (or to taste) (see page 5)	45 mL

In food processor with sharp blade attachment, process cream cheese for 2 minutes. In heavy saucepan, melt chocolate with butter over low heat. Do not overheat as chocolate will scorch. Add to food processor. Add prepared pudding, SPLENDA® Granular and fructose; process until very smooth.

Spray 2 or 3 loaf pans or one 9 x 13-inch (3 L) pan (depending on how thick the chocolate is preferred) with nonstick cooking spray. Pour into pans; cover surface with plastic wrap and store in freezer. When chocolate firms up, if desired, score into 77 squares per loaf pan. To serve, let pan stand at room temperature for 5 minutes for easier cutting.

Yield: 231 squares.

Variations: Add raisins, coconut, chopped peanuts, almonds or any nuts of your choice to the soft chocolate mixture. For richer chocolate, use 2% milk when preparing the pudding and regular cream cheese.

---

4 squares:
28 calories, 0.8 g protein, 2 g fat, 2.4 g carbohydrate, 0.4 g fiber
½ ▲ + 1 ⊞

Truffles

My husband, Ian, polished off almost all of these in one sitting!
Graham crumbs may be replaced with Grape-Nuts cereal, finely ground, or
skim milk powder (for a gluten-free treat). These truffles may be rolled in
cocoa instead of the coconut coating, if desired. (Pictured opposite page 61.)

⅔ cup	light cream cheese (see page 5)	150 mL
⅓ cup	graham crumbs	75 mL
⅓ cup	chopped pitted dates	75 mL
⅓ cup	dark seedless raisins	75 mL
3 tbsp	SPLENDA® Granular	45 mL
½ tsp	rum extract	2 mL
Chocolate Coating:		
¼ cup	all-fruit grape spread (see page 5)	50 mL
2 tbsp	cocoa	25 mL
Coconut Coating:		
⅔ cup	unsweetened medium-flaked coconut	150 mL
¼ cup	SPLENDA® Granular	50 mL

In food processor with sharp blade, process cream cheese, graham crumbs, dates, raisins, SPLENDA® Granular and rum extract until fruit is quite finely chopped.

Chocolate Coating: In small bowl, stir grape spread with cocoa.

Coconut Coating: On plate, stir the coconut with SPLENDA® Granular.

Shape truffle mixture into 1-inch (2.5 cm) balls. Roll balls in chocolate, then in coconut until well covered and no longer sticky. Place on plate; refrigerate.

Yield: 20 truffles.

---

1 truffle:
69 calories, 1.2 g protein, 4.0 g fat, 8.0 g carbohydrate, 0.7 g fiber
½ 🔾 + 1 ▲ + 1 ⊞

(clockwise from left) Nanaimo
Custard Slice (p. 108), Festive
Cranberry Pecan Squares (p. 105), and
Strawberry Almond Twirls (p. 101)

Chocolate Fudge Chews

My sons loved this chocolate and Daniel aptly named it.

6 oz	unsweetened chocolate	170 g
6 tbsp	butter or margarine, melted	90 mL
¼ cup	evaporated milk	50 mL
2 cups	SPLENDA® Granular	500 mL
1 cup	skim milk powder	250 mL
6 tbsp	granulated fructose (see page 5)	90 mL
½ tsp	vanilla extract	2 mL
⅓ cup	chopped nuts	75 mL

In heavy-bottomed saucepan over low heat or in double boiler, melt chocolate. In blender, combine butter, milk, SPLENDA® Granular, milk powder, fructose and vanilla; blend until smooth. Stir into chocolate. Stir in nuts.

Spread evenly in 8-inch (2 L) square waxed paper-lined cake pan. Freeze for 30 minutes, cover and refrigerate. Score into 10 x 10 equal divisions.

Yield: 100 pieces.

---

2 pieces:
50 calories, 1.0 g protein, 3.8 g fat, 4.4 g carbohydrate, 0.6 g fiber
½ ✳ + ½ ▲

Delicious Apple Butter (p. 117) and
Raspberry Jam (p. 119)

Apricot Balls

Brighten a tray of confections with these. (Pictured opposite page 61.)

1 cup	dried apricots	250 mL
⅓ cup	SPLENDA® Granular	75 mL
1 tbsp	finely grated orange rind	15 mL
1 tbsp	orange juice	15 mL
¾ cup	unsweetened, medium-flaked coconut	175 mL
3 tbsp	SPLENDA® Granular	45 mL
2 tbsp	unsweetened medium coconut	25 mL
1½ tsp	SPLENDA® Granular	7 mL

In food processor with sharp blade, process apricots until coarsely chopped. Add ⅓ cup (75 mL) SPLENDA® Granular, orange rind and orange juice; process until apricots are finely chopped. In small bowl, combine ¾ cup (175 mL) coconut and 3 tbsp (45 mL) SPLENDA® Granular; add to apricot mixture and process until well combined.

On plate, stir 2 tbsp (25 mL) coconut with 1½ tsp (7 mL) SPLENDA® Granular. Shape apricot mixture into 1-inch (2.5 cm) balls; roll lightly in coconut mixture. Refrigerate, uncovered, for at least 3 hours or until firm.

Yield: 22 balls.

---

1 ball:
41 calories, 0.5 g protein, 2.3 g fat, 5.3 g carbohydrate, 0.7 g fiber
½ 🔳 + ½ 🔺

Cranberry Raisins

Affectionately known as the raisins of the '90s, these dried, sweetened cranberries are great as a light snack or used in baking recipes such as muffins and quick breads. Remember that store-bought cranberry raisins are full of sugar.

1	pkg (340 g) frozen unsweetened cranberries, slightly thawed	1
Syrup:		
1¾ cups	SPLENDA® Granular	425 mL
1 cup	frozen unsweetened apple juice concentrate	250 mL
¼ cup	granulated fructose (see page 5)	50 mL
1 tbsp	cornstarch	15 mL
⅛ tsp	salt	0.5 mL
1 tbsp	butter or margarine	15 mL
1 tsp	vanilla extract	5 mL

Using scissors, cut cranberries in half; place in medium-size bowl.

Syrup: In small saucepan, stir together SPLENDA® Granular, apple juice concentrate, fructose, cornstarch, salt and butter; bring to boil, stirring. Remove from heat. Stir in vanilla. Pour over cranberries. Cover and refrigerate for 48 hours. Drain lightly.

Spray cookie sheet with nonstick cooking spray. Spread cranberries on sheet. Bake in 200°F (100°C) oven for 4½ hours, stirring after 2 hours. Turn off oven; leave cranberries inside until cool.

Leave cranberries uncovered in cool, dry place for 1 day or until preferred dryness. (Smaller berries will dry out first; they will be dehydrated and wrinkled, but still soft and pliable.) Store in small covered plastic container or sealed plastic bag at room temperature for up to 2 weeks. Refrigerate or freeze no longer than 2 months.

Yield: 1¾ cups (425 mL), 2 tbsp (25 mL) per serving.

---

2 tbsp:
35 calories, 0.1 g protein, 0.3 g fat, 8.2 g carbohydrate, 1.0 g fiber
½ 🥛 + 1 ➕

No-Bake Cookies

So easy, children aged 12 or over can make these with minimal supervision. Children love these cookies.

3 cups	quick-cooking rolled oats	750 mL
½ cup	chopped almonds or walnuts	125 mL
½ cup	unsweetened medium-flaked coconut	125 mL
⅓ cup	cocoa	75 mL
⅛ tsp	salt	0.5 mL
2¼ cups	SPLENDA® Granular	550 mL
½ cup	skim milk	125 mL
½ cup	butter or margarine	125 mL
1 tsp	vanilla extract	5 mL

In large bowl, combine oats, almonds, coconut, cocoa and salt. In saucepan, combine SPLENDA® Granular, milk and butter; bring to boil over medium heat, stirring occasionally. Remove from heat. Stir in vanilla. Pour over oat mixture; stir to combine well.

Line cookie sheet with waxed paper. Drop teaspoonfuls (5 mL) of the mixture onto paper. Refrigerate until firm, about 10 minutes.

Yield: 4 dozen.

---

2 cookies:
116 calories, 2.8 g protein, 7.4 g fat, 10.8 g carbohydrate, 1.6 g fiber
½ ■ + ½ ✳ + 1½ ▲

Chocolate Chip Oatmeal Cookies

These crunchy cookies look great and taste great.

1	egg	1
¾ cup	SPLENDA® Granular	175 mL
½ cup	butter or margarine, softened	125 mL
1 cup	quick-cooking rolled oats	250 mL
⅔ cup	all-purpose flour	150 mL
1 tsp	cinnamon	5 mL
½ tsp	baking soda	2 mL
⅔ cup	chocolate chips	150 mL

In bowl, beat together egg, SPLENDA® Granular and butter. In separate bowl, combine oats, flour, cinnamon and baking soda; stir into butter mixture. Stir in chocolate chips. Drop by tablespoonfuls (15 mL) onto greased cookie sheet. Bake in 350°F (180°C) oven for about 12 minutes.

Yield: 25 cookies.

Variation: Replace chocolate chips with raisins or a combination of raisins and chopped pecans.

---

1 cookie:

86 calories, 1.3 g protein, 5.8 g fat, 8.1 g carbohydrate, 0.8 g fiber

½ ▣ + 1 ▲

Marmalade Oat Cookies

Fruit and nuts abound in these good-for-you oatmeal cookies.
Store these soft cookies uncovered for crisper cookies.

¾ cup	butter or margarine, softened	175 mL
2	eggs	2
1½ cups	SPLENDA® Granular	375 mL
½ cup	skim milk	125 mL
1 tsp	vanilla extract	5 mL
2 cups	all-purpose flour	500 mL
1 tsp	baking soda	5 mL
½ tsp	salt	2 mL
2½ cups	quick-cooking rolled oats	625 mL
⅔ cup	all-fruit orange marmalade spread (see page 5) OR Orange Pineapple Marmalade (see page 120)	150 mL
½ cup	raisins	125 mL
½ cup	chopped walnuts	125 mL

In large bowl, beat together butter and eggs. Add SPLENDA® Granular; beat well. Stir in milk and vanilla. In another bowl, stir together flour, baking soda and salt; stir into butter mixture until combined. Add oats, marmalade, raisins and walnuts; mix well.

Drop by teaspoonfuls (5 mL) onto lightly greased cookie sheets. Bake in 350°F (180°C) oven for 12 minutes or until lightly browned underneath.

Yield: 5½ dozen cookies.

---

2 cookies:
126 calories, 2.8 g protein, 6.2 g fat, 15.6 g carbohydrate, 1.2 g fiber
1 ■ + 1 ▲

Apricot Cookies

This great recipe was given to me by a very dear friend, Mary Converse of Great Falls, Montana.

2 cups	**dried apricots**	**500 mL**
1 cup	**SPLENDA® Granular**	**250 mL**
Dough:		
3 cups	**all-purpose flour**	**750 mL**
⅓ cup	**SPLENDA® Granular**	**75 mL**
¼ tsp	**salt**	**1 mL**
8 oz	**light cream cheese, softened (see page 5)**	**250 g**
1 cup	**butter, softened**	**250 mL**

Chop apricots into ¼-inch (5 mm) pieces. In heavy-bottomed saucepan, combine apricots with SPLENDA® Granular. Add just enough water to cover apricots. Cook over medium heat, uncovered, about 30 minutes or until water has evaporated and apricots are softened.

Dough: In bowl, combine flour, SPLENDA® Granular and salt. In food processor with dough blade, process cream cheese with butter until blended. Add dry ingredients. Process on medium speed until ball forms.

Divide dough into small portions. On lightly floured surface, roll out portions, one at a time, to ⅛-inch (3 mm) thickness. Using 3-inch (8 cm) round cookie cutter with decorative wavy edge, cut out cookies. Roll up remaining dough and add another small portion to it. Repeat to use all dough.

Place ½ tsp (2 mL) apricot filling on each round; fold over 2 opposite sides to center, pinching to seal. Place on ungreased nonstick cookie sheet about 1 inch (2.5 cm) apart. Bake in 350°F (180°C) oven for 12 to 15 minutes or until golden brown underneath. Remove cookies and cool on wire racks.

Yield: 6 dozen cookies.

---

1 cookie:

60 calories, 1.0 g protein, 3.4 g fat, 6.8 g carbohydrate, 0.5 g fiber

½ ◆ + ½ ▲

Tangy Lemon Creams

Soft cookies that taste great, even without the icing. Only add icing to cookies which will be consumed the same day. For crisper cookies, leave out uncovered overnight and add icing just before serving.

½ cup	butter or margarine, softened	125 mL
2 cups	all-purpose flour	500 mL
1¼ cups	SPLENDA® Granular	300 mL
½ cup	light sour cream	125 mL
2	egg whites	2
2 tbsp	finely grated lemon rind	25 mL
1 tsp	baking powder	5 mL
¼ tsp	baking soda	1 mL
Tangy Lemon Cream Cheese Icing:		
2 tbsp	low-fat cottage cheese	25 mL
4 oz	light cream cheese (see page 5)	125 g
⅓ cup	SPLENDA® Granular	75 mL
2 tbsp	lemon juice	25 mL
2 tsp	finely grated lemon rind	10 mL
1	drop yellow food coloring	1

In food processor fitted with dough blade, process butter briefly. Add 1 cup (250 mL) of the flour; process to blend. Add remaining flour, SPLENDA® Granular, sour cream, egg whites, lemon rind, baking powder and baking soda; process on low speed until soft ball forms, increasing speed slightly after 1 minute and scraping down sides of bowl occasionally.

Drop by well-rounded teaspoonfuls (5 mL) onto ungreased cookie sheet. Flatten with back of spoon to 2-inch (5 cm) rounds. Bake in 375°F (190°C) oven for 8 to 10 minutes. Cool on wire rack. Store in sealed cookie jar.

Tangy Lemon Cream Cheese Icing: In food processor or blender with sharp blade, process cottage cheese until smooth. Add cream cheese, SPLENDA® Granular, lemon juice, lemon rind and yellow food coloring; process until smooth. Spread over cookies to be eaten same day; refrigerate remaining icing.

Yield: 48 cookies.

---

2 cookies:
100 calories, 2.4 g protein, 5.4 g fat, 10.6 g carbohydrate, 0.4 g fiber
½ ■ + ½ ✳ + 1 ▲

Strawberry Almond Twirls

Make two batches of these pretty cookies, using two different fruit spreads, and arrange in a lined attractive cookie tin, for a thoughtful gift. (Pictured opposite page 92.)

½ cup	margarine, softened	125 mL
2¾ cups	all-purpose flour	675 mL
1⅓ cups	SPLENDA® Granular	325 mL
⅓ cup	skim milk	75 mL
1	egg	1
½ tsp	baking powder	2 mL
½ tsp	almond or vanilla extract	2 mL
Strawberry Almond Filling:		
⅔ cup	all-fruit strawberry spread (see page 5)	150 mL
2 tsp	cornstarch	10 mL
½ cup	almonds, toasted and finely ground	125 mL
4	drops red food coloring (optional)	4

In food processor, process margarine for 1 minute. Add 1 cup (250 mL) of the flour; process briefly to mix. Add SPLENDA® Granular, skim milk, egg, baking powder and almond extract; process until mixed. Beat in remaining flour. Form into 2 balls; flatten into disks. Wrap in waxed paper or plastic wrap; chill for 1 hour.

Strawberry Almond Filling: In small saucepan, combine fruit spread with cornstarch; cook over medium heat until bubbly. Remove from heat. Stir in almonds, and red food coloring if desired. Set aside to cool.

Roll each disk into 12 x 8-inch (30 x 20 cm) rectangle, cutting and patching if necessary. Spread with filling. Using flat spatula to lift dough, roll up fairly tightly from long side, jelly-roll style. For larger cookies, roll from short side. Wrap each roll in waxed paper. Refrigerate 2 to 12 hours.

Using sharp knife, cut into ¼-inch (5 mm) thick slices. Place on greased foil-lined cookie sheets. Bake in 375°F (190°C) oven for 9 to 11 minutes or until light brown underneath. Remove cookies and cool on wire racks.

Yield: 52 small cookies or 44 large cookies.

---

1 small cookie:
52 calories, 1.1 g protein, 2.3 g fat, 6.7 g carbohydrate, 0.3 g fiber
½ ◼ + ½ ▲

Brownies

A moist, dense, delicious brownie.

4	egg whites	4
½ cup	unsweetened applesauce	125 mL
⅓ cup	vegetable oil	75 mL
¼ cup	all-fruit grape spread (see page 5)	50 mL
2 tsp	vanilla extract	10 mL
1½ cups	SPLENDA® Granular	375 mL
1¼ cups	all-purpose flour	300 mL
½ cup	cocoa	125 mL
¼ tsp	salt	1 mL
	Chocolate Fudge Topping, page 111	

In large bowl, beat egg whites until frothy; beat in applesauce, oil, grape spread and vanilla. In separate bowl, combine SPLENDA® Granular, flour, cocoa and salt; add to egg white mixture and beat just until blended.

Scoop into greased 8-inch (2 L) square cake pan, smoothing top with knife. Bake in 350°F (180°C) oven for 20 minutes. Let cool. Glaze with Chocolate Fudge Topping. Cut into squares.

Yield: 16 brownies.

Variation: Add ⅓ cup (75 mL) chopped nuts, if desired.

---

1 brownie with topping:
135 calories, 3.4 g protein, 6.7 g fat, 17.3 g carbohydrate, 2.4 g fiber
1 ■ + 1½ ▲

Strawberry Jelly Squares

Beautiful, delicious squares! Only problem is they disappear too quickly!

Crust:

1¼ cups	all-purpose flour	300 mL
¼ cup	SPLENDA® Granular	50 mL
6 tbsp	butter or margarine, melted	90 mL

Cream Cheese Filling:

8 oz	light cream cheese (see page 5)	250 g
⅔ cup	SPLENDA® Granular Condensed Milk, page 114	150 mL
1	pkg (30 g) light vanilla pudding mix (see page 5)	1
¼ cup	skim milk	50 mL
¼ cup	water	50 mL
1 tsp	vanilla extract	5 mL

Strawberry Jelly Topping:

27	small fresh strawberries, halved	27
2	pkg (11 g each) low-calorie strawberry gelatin	2
2 cups	boiling water	500 mL

Crust: In small bowl, combine flour and SPLENDA® Granular; stir in butter with fork. Press firmly into 9 x 13-inch (23 x 33 cm) baking dish. Bake in 350°F (180°C) oven for 10 to 15 minutes or until slightly browned. Allow to cool.

Cream Cheese Filling: In bowl, beat cream cheese with SPLENDA® Granular Condensed Milk until smooth. Add remaining ingredients; beat on low speed for 2 to 3 minutes, scraping bowl occasionally. Spread carefully over cooled crust.

Strawberry Jelly Topping: Place strawberry halves over filling in 6 rows down and 9 columns across. Refrigerate 30 minutes. Dissolve strawberry gelatin in boiling water. Allow to cool to room temperature; pour over filling. Refrigerate until firm.

Yield: 54 squares.

---

1 square:
50 calories, 1.4 g protein, 2.8 g fat, 4.6 g carbohydrate, 0.3 g fiber
½ ■ + ½ ▲

Butter Tart Squares

Firmer in texture than traditional butter tart squares. This crust works very well with cheesecakes (see nutritional analysis below and Helpful Hints, page 3).

Short Crust:

1 cup	all-purpose flour	250 mL
3 tbsp	SPLENDA® Granular	45 mL
⅛ tsp	salt	0.5 mL
⅓ cup	butter, melted	75 mL

Topping:

2	eggs	2
1 tbsp	butter, melted	15 mL
1 tsp	vanilla extract	5 mL
1 cup	SPLENDA® Granular	250 mL
2 tbsp	all-purpose flour	25 mL
½ tsp	cinnamon	2 mL
¼ tsp	baking powder	1 mL
⅛ tsp	salt	0.5 mL
1 cup	golden raisins	250 mL

Short Crust: In small bowl, combine flour, SPLENDA® Granular and salt; stir in butter well with fork. Press into 8-inch (2 L) square cake pan. Bake in 350°F (180°C) oven for 10 minutes.

Topping: In bowl, beat eggs with fork; stir in butter and vanilla. In separate bowl, combine SPLENDA® Granular, flour, cinnamon, baking powder and salt; stir into egg mixture. Stir in raisins. Spread over baked crust. Bake in 350°F (180°C) oven for 15 to 20 minutes or until slightly browned at edges and just softly set.

Yield: 25 squares.

---

1 square:
76 calories, 1.3 g protein, 3.4 g fat, 10.5 g carbohydrate, 0.6 g fiber
1 ⬛ + ½ ▲

1 serving Short Crust (for cheesecakes) = 1/12 of recipe:
85 calories, 1.1 g protein, 5.2 g fat, 8.0 g carbohydrate, 0.3 g fiber
½ ⬛ + 1 ▲

Festive Cranberry Pecan Squares

These moist and fruity squares freeze well for holiday company.
(Pictured opposite page 92.)

1½ cups	all-purpose flour	375 mL
⅓ cup	SPLENDA® Granular	75 mL
⅛ tsp	salt	0.5 mL
½ cup	butter or margarine, melted	125 mL

Filling:

2	eggs, lightly beaten	2
1	egg white, lightly beaten	1
⅔ cup	skim milk	150 mL
1 tsp	vanilla extract	5 mL
1⅔ cups	SPLENDA® Granular	400 mL
½ cup	all-purpose flour	125 mL
1 tsp	baking powder	5 mL
¼ tsp	salt	1 mL
2 tbsp	finely grated orange rind	25 mL
1½ cups	fresh or frozen cranberries	375 mL
½ cup	unsweetened medium-flaked coconut	125 mL
½ cup	finely chopped pecans	125 mL
⅓ cup	golden raisins, coarsely chopped	75 mL

In small bowl, combine flour, SPLENDA® Granular and salt; stir in butter with fork. Press into 9 x 13-inch (23 x 33 cm) cake pan. Bake in 350°F (180°C) oven for 8 to 10 minutes.

Filling: In large bowl, combine eggs, egg white, milk and vanilla. In separate bowl, stir together SPLENDA® Granular, flour, baking powder and salt; stir in orange rind. Add to egg mixture, stirring to combine.

Chop cranberries at high speed in food processor fitted with sharp blade; fold into batter along with coconut, pecans and golden raisins. Spread evenly over baked crust. Bake in 350°F (180°C) oven for 25 minutes or until edges are light brown. While still warm, cut into squares. Cool in pan on wire rack.

Yield: 36 squares.

---

1 square:
83 calories, 1.6 g protein, 4.4 g fat, 9.6 g carbohydrate, 0.7 g fiber
½ [■] + 1 [▲]

Chocolate Coconut Squares

A moist, chewy, sweet square. Granulated fructose is available in health food stores and most larger supermarkets.

⅔ cup	SPLENDA® Granular Condensed Milk, page 114	150 mL
1½ oz	unsweetened chocolate, melted	45 g
2 tbsp	granulated fructose (see page 5)	25 mL
2 tsp	vanilla extract	10 mL
2 cups	unsweetened finely flaked coconut	500 mL
½ cup	SPLENDA® Granular	125 mL

In bowl, stir together SPLENDA® Granular Condensed Milk, chocolate, fructose and vanilla. In small bowl, stir together coconut and SPLENDA® Granular; stir into chocolate mixture until evenly distributed.

Spray 8-inch (2 L) square cake pan with nonstick cooking spray. Press mixture evenly and firmly onto bottom of pan. Refrigerate, uncovered, overnight.

Yield: 36 squares.

---

1 square:
59 calories, 1.1 g protein, 4.5 g fat, 4.3 g carbohydrate, 0.5 g fiber
½ [✽] + 1 [▲]

Lamingtons

My variation of a treat popular in South Africa and Australia. These are best eaten the same day.

2 cups	self-rising cake-and-pastry flour (see page 4)	500 mL
1 tsp	baking powder	5 mL
2	eggs	2
2	egg whites	2
1 cup	SPLENDA® Granular	250 mL
½ cup	hot pineapple juice	125 mL
3 tbsp	butter, melted	45 mL
Coconut Covering:		
1½ cups	unsweetened medium-flaked coconut	375 mL
⅓ cup	SPLENDA® Granular	75 mL
Chocolate Dip:		
1 cup	Chocolate Fudge Topping, page 111	250 mL
⅔ cup	skim milk	150 mL

In large bowl, stir together flour and baking powder. In separate bowl, beat together eggs and egg whites; beat in SPLENDA® Granular. Stir into dry ingredients with wooden spoon. In small bowl, combine pineapple juice and butter; stir into batter until well combined.

Spoon into greased 8-inch (2 L) square baking pan; smooth surface with knife. Bake in 350°F (180°C) oven for 20 minutes or until cake tester comes out clean. Run knife along edges of cake; invert onto wire rack. Remove all crusted edges with sharp knife. Cut into 25 squares.

Coconut Covering: In small bowl, combine coconut and SPLENDA® Granular.

Chocolate Dip: In heavy-bottomed saucepan or double boiler, stir Chocolate Fudge Topping with milk until very hot. Allow to cool slightly.

With fork, dip each warm cake square into chocolate to coat completely. Roll in coconut mixture. Place on wire rack until set.

Yield: 25 pieces.

---

1 piece:
114 calories, 2.9 g protein, 5.7 g fat, 13.8 g carbohydrate, 1.2 g fiber
½ ■ + ½ ✳ + 1 ▲

Nanaimo Custard Slices

So decadent, but so good! (Pictured opposite page 92.)

1 cup	graham cracker crumbs	250 mL
½ cup	SPLENDA® Granular	125 mL
⅓ cup	unsweetened medium-flaked coconut	75 mL
2 tbsp	cocoa	25 mL
¼ cup	butter, melted	50 mL
1	egg, beaten	1
Custard Layer:		
2 tsp	unflavored gelatin	10 mL
1 tbsp	cold water	15 mL
¾ cup	SPLENDA® Granular	175 mL
¼ cup	custard powder	50 mL
2 cups	2% milk	500 mL
Chocolate Layer:		
2 oz	semisweet chocolate	60 g
2 tbsp	butter	25 mL
¼ cup	SPLENDA® Granular	50 mL
2 tbsp	2% evaporated milk	25 mL

In bowl, combine graham cracker crumbs, SPLENDA® Granular, coconut and cocoa; stir in butter and egg. Press into 8-inch (2 L) square cake pan. Bake in 350°F (180°C) oven for 8 to 10 minutes. Allow to cool.

Custard Layer: In cup, stir gelatin with cold water; set aside to soften. In heavy-bottomed saucepan, combine SPLENDA® Granular and custard powder; gradually whisk in milk with wire whisk until smooth. Bring to boil over medium heat, stirring constantly. Remove from heat. Stir in softened gelatin. Cover surface with plastic wrap; set aside to cool slightly. Pour carefully over crust. Refrigerate 20 minutes or until set well, before adding next layer.

Chocolate Layer: In small saucepan, melt chocolate with butter over medium heat. Stir in SPLENDA® Granular and milk until very smooth. Spread gently over custard layer. Refrigerate.

Yield: 25 squares.

---

1 square:
87 calories, 1.8 g protein, 5.5 g fat, 8.7 g carbohydrate, 0.5 g fiber
½ ■ + 1 ▲

Pineapple Cheesecake Bars

These attractive bars could feed a crowd. Our special friends Horst and Annette and family enjoyed this dessert.

	unbaked Graham Crumb Crust for Pies, page 65	
Filling:		
2 cups	part-skim ricotta cheese	500 mL
8 oz	light cream cheese, softened (see page 5)	250 g
1	can (14 oz/398 mL) unsweetened crushed pineapple	1
2	envelopes unflavored gelatin	2
2 cups	prepared low-calorie dessert topping (see page 5)	500 mL
1 cup	SPLENDA® Granular	250 mL
1 tsp	vanilla extract	5 mL
1 tbsp	graham cracker crumbs	15 mL

Press crust into 13 x 9-inch (3 L) baking dish, but bake for only 5 minutes in 350°F (180°C) oven.

Filling: In food processor or blender with sharp blade, process ricotta cheese until smooth. Add cream cheese; beat about 1 minute on low speed.

Drain pineapple, reserving ½ cup (125 mL) juice. In small saucepan, soften gelatin in ¼ cup (50 mL) of the pineapple juice; add remaining pineapple juice and dissolve over low heat. Add to cream cheese mixture along with dessert topping, SPLENDA® Granular and vanilla. Process until smooth. Stir in pineapple. Spread over baked crust. Sprinkle with graham crumbs. Chill until firm.

Yield: 40 bars.

---

1 bar:
56 calories, 2.6 g protein, 2.8 g fat, 5.3 g carbohydrate, 0.2 g fiber
1/2 [🖊] + 1/2 [▲]

Frostings, Sauces, Butters and Jams

Strawberry Whipped Topping

This makes a delicious pale pastel pink topping. For a deeper pink use red food coloring.

4	unsweetened frozen large strawberries	4
2 cups	prepared low-calorie dessert topping (see page 5)	500 mL
⅓ cup	SPLENDA® Granular	75 mL
2 tbsp	plain yogurt	25 mL

Thaw strawberries slightly; pat dry with paper towel and chop finely. In bowl, beat together dessert topping, SPLENDA® Granular, yogurt and strawberries.

Yield: 3 cups (750 mL), 6 servings.

---

1 serving:

45 calories, 1.3 g protein, 2.1 g fat, 5.7 g carbohydrate, 0.2 g fiber

½ ✳ + ½ ▲

Chocolate Fudge Topping

This topping becomes firm in the fridge; microwave a few seconds to rectify.

2 tbsp	diet margarine	25 mL
1 cup	SPLENDA® Granular	250 mL
½ cup	cocoa	125 mL
⅓ cup	all-fruit grape spread (see page 5)	75 mL
3 tbsp	evaporated skim milk	45 mL
2 tbsp	skim milk powder	25 mL
1 tsp	vanilla extract	5 mL

In blender, combine margarine, SPLENDA® Granular, cocoa, grape spread, evaporated milk, milk powder and vanilla; blend until smooth.

In small, heavy-bottomed saucepan, cook mixture over low heat, stirring, until smooth and very hot. Use immediately or cover and refrigerate.

Yield: 1 cup (250 mL).

---

1 tbsp:

30 calories, 1.0 g protein, 1.4 g fat, 4.6 g carbohydrate, 1.0 g fiber

½ ✳

Chocolate Frosting

A sweet and creamy, rich frosting. Fructose (a fruit sugar) is available in most larger supermarkets and health food stores.

1 oz	unsweetened chocolate	30 g
3 tbsp	butter	45 mL
3 tbsp	cocoa	45 mL
½ cup	evaporated skim milk	125 mL
1 cup	SPLENDA® Granular	250 mL
⅓ cup	all-fruit grape spread (see page 5)	75 mL
¼ cup	granulated fructose (see page 5)	50 mL
3	envelopes low-calorie dessert topping mix (makes 3 cups/750 mL) (see page 5)	3
½ cup	skim milk	125 mL

In saucepan, melt chocolate with butter over medium heat; stir in cocoa. Gradually stir in evaporated milk with wire whisk. Stir in SPLENDA® Granular, grape spread and fructose; bring to boil, stirring. Pour into shallow container; cover and freeze for 1 hour.

In bowl, beat low-calorie dessert topping mix with ½ cup (125 mL) skim milk for 3 minutes or until thickened. Add chocolate mixture; beat until well combined. Frost cooled 2-layer cake immediately or refrigerate until slightly firmer (if necessary). Refrigerate cake after 1 day; let cake stand at room temperature at least 2 hours before serving.

Yield: Sufficient to fill and frost 2-layer cake (12 servings).

Variation:
Chocolate Mocha Frosting: Add 2 tsp (10 mL) instant coffee granules simultaneously with cocoa.

---

1 serving:
102 calories, 1.9 g protein, 5.7 g fat, 12.4 g carbohydrate, 0.6 g fiber
1 ✳ + 1 ▲

Creamy Butter Icings

Refrigerate icings, when necessary, until firmer. For "drizzling" consistency, use diet margarine, instead of butter. The Canadian Diabetes Association Food Choice Values and/or Symbols will be the same for White, Maple, Pink, Mocha and Lemon Icings.

White Icing:

⅔ cup	SPLENDA® Granular Condensed Milk, page 114 (made with softened butter)	150 mL
4	envelopes low-calorie dessert topping mix (each makes 1 cup/250 mL) (see page 5)	4
⅓ cup	skim milk	75 mL

White Icing: Prepare SPLENDA® Granular Condensed Milk using softened butter instead of diet margarine. Set aside.

In bowl, beat 3 of the envelopes dessert topping mix with skim milk until thickened. Add SPLENDA® Granular Condensed Milk and remaining envelope of dessert topping mix; beat 3 minutes on high speed. Frost 2-layer cake and serve at room temperature. Leave the cake, covered, outside the fridge for a maximum of 2 days.

Yield: Sufficient to fill and frost 2-layer cake (12 servings)

Variations:

Maple Icing: Beat in ¾ tsp (4 mL) maple extract, or to taste.

Pink Icing: Beat in red food coloring, 1 drop at a time, until desired color.

Mocha Icing: Dissolve 1½ tsp (7 mL) instant coffee granules in 1 tbsp (15 mL) hot water; beat into icing.

Orange Butter Icing: Beat in 4 tbsp (60 mL) frozen orange juice concentrate and ½ tsp (2 mL) orange extract. Add 2 drops yellow food coloring and 1 red for an orange hue.

Lemon Butter Icing: Beat in 3 tbsp (45 mL) lemon juice and ¼ tsp (1 mL) lemon extract. Add 2 drops yellow food coloring.

Chocolate Butter Icing: Beat in ⅓ cup (75 mL) cocoa and ¼ cup (50 mL) SPLENDA® Granular, OR 1 oz (30 g) melted bittersweet chocolate.

Chocolate Almond Icing: Prepare chocolate icing above and beat in ½ tsp (2 mL) almond extract.

---

1 serving White Icing:
72 calories, 2.5 g protein, 3.8 g fat, 7.2 g carbohydrate, 0 g fiber
½ ◆ Skim + ½ ✳ + ½ ▲

SPLENDA® Granular Condensed Milk

This useful recipe was given to me by my friend, Donna Champion, who was baking Christmas cookies at the time. I adapted it, making it lower in fat and calories.

1 cup	skim milk powder	250 mL
1 cup	SPLENDA® Granular	250 mL
¼ cup	diet margarine	50 mL
¼ cup	water	50 mL

In blender, blend milk powder, SPLENDA® Granular, margarine and water until smooth, scraping down sides to incorporate all dry ingredients.

Yield: ⅔ cup (150 mL).

---

1 batch:

536 calories, 24.2 g protein, 22.5 g fat, 59.5 g carbohydrate, 0 g fiber

6 ◆ Skim + 2½ ✳ + 4½ ▲

Peach Sauce

So quick and easy.

1	can (14 oz/398 mL) unsweetened sliced peaches in juice	1
¼ cup	SPLENDA® Granular	50 mL
½ tsp	vanilla extract	2 mL

In blender, blend together peaches, SPLENDA® Granular and vanilla until smooth.

Yield: 2 cups (500 mL), ¼ cup (50 mL) per serving.

Variation: Spiced Pear Sauce: Substitute canned pears for the peaches. Omit vanilla extract. Add ½ tsp (2 mL) ground ginger.

---

1 serving:

27 calories, 0.3 g protein, 0 g fat, 6.9 g carbohydrate, 0.5 g fiber

½ ◐

Rhubarb Sauce

Serve warm over Vanilla Ice Cream, page 85, or with Rhubarb Coffee Cake, page 39.

9 cups	cut up (½-inch/2 cm pieces) rhubarb	2.25 L
1½ cups	SPLENDA® Granular	375 mL
¾ cup	orange juice	175 mL
2 tbsp	finely grated orange rind (optional)	25 mL
1½ tbsp	cornstarch	22 mL
2	drops red food coloring (optional)	2

In saucepan, stir together rhubarb, SPLENDA® Granular, orange juice, orange rind, if desired, and cornstarch; bring to boil over medium high heat, stirring occasionally. Reduce heat to minimum; simmer, covered, 12 to 15 minutes or until rhubarb is soft. Stir in red food coloring, if desired.

Yield: 5 cups (1.25 L), ½ cup (125 mL) per serving.

---

1 serving:
50 calories, 1.1 g protein, 0.2 g fat, 11.6 g carbohydrate, 2.0 g fiber
1 🍃

Rum Custard Sauce

Serve chilled with fresh fruit or serve warm over a slice of coffee cake.

¼ cup	SPLENDA® Granular	50 mL
3 tbsp	custard powder	45 mL
2 cups	skim milk	500 mL
1 tbsp	diet margarine	15 mL
1 tsp	rum extract	5 mL

In small bowl, mix together SPLENDA® Granular, custard powder and ¼ cup (50 mL) of the milk. In heavy-bottomed saucepan, bring remaining milk to boil; remove from heat. Stir in custard mixture and continue stirring until thickened. Stir in margarine and rum extract. Serve warm or cover surface with plastic wrap and refrigerate. Blend chilled sauce until smooth in blender before serving.

Yield: 2 cups (500 mL), ¼ cup (50 mL) per serving.

---

1 serving:
43 calories, 2.1 g protein, 0.8 g fat, 6.5 g carbohydrate, 0 g fiber
½ ◆ Skim + ½ ✳

Vanilla-Flavored Syrup

Pour this syrup over pancakes, crêpes, waffles or ice cream. Fructose is a pure fruit sugar, available in larger supermarkets and health food stores.

3½ cups	SPLENDA® Granular	875 mL
2 cups	water	500 mL
½ cup	granulated fructose (see page 5)	125 mL
2 tbsp	cornstarch	25 mL
2 tbsp	butter or margarine	25 mL
¼ tsp	salt	1 mL
2 tsp	vanilla extract	10 mL

In saucepan, combine SPLENDA® Granular, water, fructose, cornstarch, butter and salt; bring to boil, stirring with wire whisk occasionally. Reduce heat, cover and simmer for 2 minutes. Remove from heat; stir in vanilla. Store syrup in covered container in fridge; to serve again, stir with wire whisk and heat slightly in microwave oven.

Yield: 2½ cups (625 mL).

Variations:

Maple-Flavored Syrup: Substitute maple extract for vanilla extract.

Butterscotch-Flavored Syrup: Substitute butterscotch extract for vanilla extract.

---

1 tbsp:
25 calories, 0 g protein, 0.6 g fat, 5.0 g carbohydrate, 0 g fiber
½ ✱

Delicious Apple Butter Spread

This spread is wonderful on hot buttered toast, toasted English muffins or toasted bagels. (Pictured opposite page 93.)

1	can (14 oz/398 mL) unsweetened applesauce	1
¼ cup	unsweetened frozen apple juice concentrate	50 mL
¼ cup	SPLENDA® Granular	50 mL
½ tsp	cinnamon	2 mL
¼ tsp	ground cloves	1 mL
¼ tsp	salt	1 mL

In heavy-bottomed saucepan, stir together applesauce, apple juice concentrate, SPLENDA® Granular, cinnamon, cloves and salt. Boil over medium-low heat, partially covered, 40 to 50 minutes or until thick, stirring occasionally. Refrigerate in closed container for up to 3 weeks.

Yield: 1⅓ cups (325 mL).

---

1 tbsp:
15 calories, 0.1 g protein, 0 g fat, 3.8 g carbohydrate, 0.3 g fiber
½ 🍎

Cinnamon Butter

Wonderful for spreading on toast, hot muffins or loaves.

1 cup	SPLENDA® Granular	250 mL
⅓ cup	soft margarine (not diet)	75 mL
3 tbsp	skim milk	45 mL
2 tsp	cinnamon (or to taste)	10 mL

In food processor, combine SPLENDA® Granular, margarine, milk and cinnamon; process on lowest speed until smooth, scraping down sides of bowl occasionally.

Yield: ⅔ cup (150 mL).

---

1 tbsp:
62 calories, 0.2 g protein, 5.7 g fat, 2.8 g carbohydrate, 0.1 g fiber
½ ✱ + 1 ▲

Apricot Jam

This jam tastes deliciously tart (see Helpful Hints, page 5).

6 cups	finely chopped unpeeled apricots	1.5 L
3 tbsp	lemon juice	45 mL
3 cups	SPLENDA® Granular	750 mL
1	pkg (57 g) sugarless powdered Fruit Pectin (see page 5)	1
½ tsp	butter	2 mL
1 tbsp	unflavored gelatin	15 mL
1 tbsp	cold water	15 mL

Cover four 1-cup (250 mL) jars, lids and pair of tongs with boiling water to sterilize.

In large kettle, combine apricots with lemon juice. Add SPLENDA® Granular and stir in well. Stir in pectin. Bring to full rolling boil over high heat, stirring constantly. Add butter. Boil for 1 minute. Remove from heat. Skim off foam with spoon. Meanwhile, soften gelatin in cold water; stir into jam until dissolved. Immediately fill and seal sterilized jars, leaving ½-inch (1 cm) headspace. Refrigerate or freeze up to 1 year.

Yield: 4 cups (1 L).

Variations:

Strawberry Jam: Substitute frozen unsweetened thawed strawberries, crushed or ground for the apricots. (Fresh sliced strawberries may be substituted in season. Add a few drops red food coloring for a deeper red color if you're using fresh strawberries.) Omit lemon juice.

Peach Jam: Substitute finely chopped peeled fresh peaches for the apricots.

---

1 tbsp:
15 calories, 0.3 g protein, 0.1 g fat, 3.6 g carbohydrate, 0.3 g fiber
½ 🖊

Raspberry Jam

This ruby red jam becomes quite addictive. I have raspberry bushes growing in my garden and this is a favorite summertime recipe. (Pictured opposite page 93.)

5 cups	raspberries	1.25 L
1 cup	frozen unsweetened apple juice concentrate	250 mL
2 cups	SPLENDA® Granular	500 mL
1	pkg (57 g) sugarless powdered Fruit Pectin (see page 5)	1
½ tsp	butter	2 mL
1	envelope unflavored gelatin	1
1 tbsp	cold water	15 mL

Cover four 1-cup (250 mL) jars, lids and pair of tongs with boiling water to sterilize.

In large kettle, crush raspberries. Add apple juice concentrate. Stir in SPLENDA® Granular. Stir in pectin. Bring to full rolling boil over medium-high heat, stirring constantly. Add butter. Boil, stirring, for 1 minute.

Remove from heat. Skim off any foam, if necessary. Meanwhile, soften gelatin in cold water; stir into jam until dissolved. Immediately fill and seal sterilized jars, leaving ½ inch (1 cm) headspace. Refrigerate for up to 1 year.

Yield: 3¾ cups (925 mL).

Variations:

Blueberry Jam: Substitute fresh or frozen, thawed blueberries for the raspberries. Add 2 tbsp (25 mL) lemon juice.

Strawberry Jam: Substitute sliced fresh or frozen, unsweetened, almost thawed strawberries for the raspberries. Increase gelatin to 1½ envelopes and dissolve in 2 tbsp (25 mL) cold water. (This is a sweeter, smoother jam, than the Strawberry Jam recipe, page 118.)

---

1 tbsp Raspberry Jam:
19 calories, 0.2 g protein, 0.1 g fat, 4.6 g carbohydrate, 0.5 g fiber
½ 🗩

Orange Pineapple Marmalade

You're in for a treat with this lovely jam and it is so easy to prepare.
Make this marmalade any time of the year.

2	oranges	2
1	12 oz (355 mL) can frozen unsweetened concentrated pineapple juice, thawed	1
2 cups	SPLENDA® Granular	500 mL
1	pkg (57 g) sugarless powdered Fruit Pectin (see page 5)	1
¼ tsp	butter	1 mL

Cut both ends off oranges, removing any hard areas. Cut oranges into quarters; scoop out pulp. Remove any seeds. Chop pulp quite finely. Cut peel into match-stick thin slices, about ½ inch (1 cm) long.

In large saucepan, bring pulp, peel and 2 cups (500 mL) water to boil; reduce heat, cover and simmer about 1 hour or until peel is soft. Measure out 2 cups (500 mL) into large kettle. Add water to pineapple concentrate to equal 2 cups (500 mL); stir into fruit mixture. Stir in SPLENDA® Granular. Add fruit pectin; stir to combine. Bring to full rolling boil over medium-high heat, stirring constantly. Add butter; boil, stirring, for 1 minute.

Remove from heat. Wait 30 seconds; skim off any foam. Immediately fill and seal hot sterilized jars, leaving ½ inch (1 cm) headspace. Refrigerate for up to 1 year.

Yield: 3¼ cups (800 mL).

Note: Preparing jars: Jars should have been washed in a dishwasher at some point. Rinse if they have been standing on the shelf a long time. Pour boiling water over everything, making sure to fill all the jars completely. Pour boiling water over any spoons, tongs, lids and rings that will be used. Let everything sit in the hot water until they're needed. Use the tongs to pick up the jars and invert to remove the water and to pick up lids and rings.

---

1 tbsp:
24 calories, 0.2 g protein, 0 g fat, 6.2 g carbohydrate, 0.4 g fiber
½ 🍩

Index